# LIVE THE WORLD YOU WANT

## A Handbook for Students of Life

### By

### Clay Boland Jr.

ISBN: 1-4033-1722-4 (e-book)
ISBN: 1-4033-1723-2 (Paperback)

This book is printed on acid free paper.

Graphics by Rich Frank

1stBooks - rev. 09/14/05

# TABLE OF CONTENTS

**SECTION V: MAKING THE MOST OF IT**

# PREFACE

*"The greatest art of all is the art of life, for it is not only the most challenging of all the arts, but it is also the only art available to each and every one of us. To make of our individual lives the outstanding 'works of art' they can be, and to make of our brief sojourns in this world with others the 'works of art' they should be, are artistic endeavors available to one and all."*

-- *"Art and Existence," p. 143*

This is a handbook that invites you to participate in doing something about the state of the world primarily by exemplifying in your own life the way you want the world to be.

And since most people desire to live life fully and with meaning and self-respect, this is a handbook about making the most out of the gift of life for yourself and for others.

Unless you first get yourself together, you cannot get together with anyone else, and you cannot help any of us get together.

If you are not living up to your own potential, you have no right to complain about the rest of humankind falling short of doing the same. If you live up to your own potential, or at least more of your potential than you are living up to at present, you will be helping others do the same; you will be helping create, within the sphere of your own influence, a better world because of your presence in it.

This is a handbook that promotes neither the advancement of the individual at the expense of the group nor the advancement of the group at the expense of the individual. History has shown again and again that either imbalance eventually fails through the dissatisfaction of the disenfranchised, whether it be the group or the individual.

This is a handbook that promotes the development of the potential of the individual as the key to the development of the potential of the group, for the group can be stronger and more invincible but never significantly better than the individuals who are its members.

War and peace start with the individual. When more people are more at peace with themselves and those around them, there will be more peace in the world. But if more people are more at war with themselves and those around them, there will be more war in the world. The individual counts. The individual is the most potent and the least recognized source of change. And I am not referring to the famous and infamous individuals whose autobiographies and biographies can be found in your local library—individuals who, most would agree, have changed the world for better or for worse—but to the anonymous individuals who have also changed and continue to change the world for better or for worse whether they realize it or not. For the world, in as far as humankind affects it, is the result of all the individual thoughts, words, and actions of all of the people who inhabit it and of all those who have inhabited it before them.

This is a handbook for students of life who, loving wisdom, wish to use that wisdom to create a better world for themselves and others; and who are willing to do this primarily by "living the world they want" as the first, and perhaps most important, step toward helping bring about that better world.

This handbook invites you to join them.

# LIVE THE WORLD YOU WANT

IF YOU WANT PEOPLE TO BE LOVING,
BE LOVING;
IF YOU WANT PEOPLE TO BE UNDERSTANDING,
BE UNDERSTANDING;
IF YOU WANT PEOPLE TO INVEST THEMSELVES
IN RELATIONSHIPS
AND
MAKE AN EFFORT
TO MAKE THEM WORK,
INVEST YOURSELF;

IF YOU WANT A WORLD IN WHICH PEOPLE ARE LESS
GREEDY, SHARE;
IF YOU WANT A WORLD WITH LESS WAR,
BE MORE AT PEACE WITH YOURSELF
AND
OTHERS;
IF YOU WANT A WORLD IN WHICH MORE PEOPLE
CONTRIBUTE, GIVE;

IF YOU WANT A BETTER WORLD,
BE A BETTER PERSON.

EVEN IF OTHERS DO OTHERWISE,
YOU CAN KNOW
THAT YOU ARE DOING
WHAT YOU CAN DO
TO MAKE THE WORLD
A BIT BETTER
RATHER THAN WORSE;

FOR THE WORLD IS SIMPLY YOU AND I MULTIPLIED,
AND MULTIPLIED,
THROUGHOUT TIME
AND IS NO BETTER
OR WORSE
THAN YOU AND I MAKE IT.

# SECTION I: THE GIFT

*Clay Boland Jr.*

# THE UNGRATEFUL LIVING

> *"The great event of all history, of all time, the humble, artless truth of mere being...the glorious truth of mere being."*
> —William Saroyan

Life, however difficult and confusing, is an incredible and miraculous event that should fill each one of us living in reasonable health and circumstances with wonder and gratitude every day we are privileged to enjoy it. And yet, many of us depreciate life by taking it for granted—as if it is common, and ordinary, and, in some sense, our due.

Far too many of us, for example, take seeing, hearing, tasting, touching, smelling, and the ability to talk or walk as things of little or no value; and consider the whole panorama of nature's infinite variety and beauty as an insignificant stage set, a mere backdrop for our personal, earth-shaking dramas, each titled, THE UNIVERSE, STARRING ME.

Worse yet, most of us, through our ingratitude, create endless discontent in our lives. Rather than being grateful for what we have, *we worry about what we don't have or about what we have that we don't want* (even though it may be the best thing for us). And so, living in the midst of a paradise of plenty, we create the discomforts of purgatory and sometimes even the pains of hell, and try to escape into temporary limbo as often as possible. We have done the medieval theologians one better. They envisioned such

3

punishments as occurring after life. We seem determined to "enjoy" them while we are still living.

Why not try a little gratitude?

You'll be thankful you did.

Not tomorrow, when things are better;

But today, to make things better.

Don't wait until you're dead to be grateful;

Join the grateful living.

NOW.

## DEFERRED LIVING

SOME PEOPLE PAY NOW
AND NEVER FLY.

THEY BUY TICKET AFTER TICKET AFTER TICKET
BUT ARE ALWAYS TOO BUSY TO BOARD.

WHEN THEY FINALLY GET TO THE TERMINAL,
THEY FRANTICALLY RUSH TO THE GATE

ONLY TO DISCOVER THAT THEIR PLANE
HAS TAKEN OFF WITHOUT THEM,

AND ALL OTHER FLIGHTS
HAVE BEEN CANCELLED FOREVER.

# DAILY THANKSGIVING

> *"Hush, hush, Whisper*
> *who dares! Christopher Robin*
> *is saying his prayers."*
> —*A. A. Milne*

Many people have claimed to have heard voices directing them towards certain actions. I suppose most of us have had similar experiences, even though we are pretty sure that such voices were nothing more than good old common sense getting us back on the right track again.

For a number of years I have reestablished my childhood custom of kneeling down at my bedside to say some prayers before going to sleep. I often feel somewhat funny about this, being sufficiently embarrassed enough to be sure that my wife does not witness this recidivism to my Christopher Robin days, but I find it comforting and helpful.

Recently, all these prayers seem to start in the same vein, that of thanksgiving—thanksgiving for all the gifts of the day, thanksgiving for all that I have been lucky enough to experience and receive.

But no sooner do I start my thanksgiving than a voice within, the exact source of which I leave to others to identify, immediately stops me with a simple statement: *"If you are really thankful, show it. The words you say are empty tokens of gratitude. The best way to prove that you are grateful is to live your thanksgiving. Pass the gratitude on to others in your life. Live your thanks."*

And so, the next day I live my prayer—and I don't have to be at all embarrassed about it, for "something tells me" it's the right thing to do.

# LIVING LIFE

> *"Happiness comes of the grace to accept life gratefully and make the best of it."*
> —*Donald C. Peattie*

Life, as most of us understand it, takes place in a space-time continuum. Although mystics and other transcendental thinkers may argue that both space and time are illusions, both are real enough for most people.

This life may be but a movie, as Richard Bach suggests in his book, *Illusions,* but most of us believe the fleeting images contain all the reality we could possibly wish to bear, and many of us wish for more than the normal fifty percent of darkness (i.e., forgetfulness) shown on the screen during the film.

Some scientific thinkers propose that we are only collections of vibrations, and although this hypothesis is becoming easier and easier to prove with the help of modern physics, most of us are still constantly, as when one of us stubs a toe, convinced of the reality of "this too, too solid flesh."

Others have said that life is a dream from which we will eventually awake. However, most of us suspect strongly that whether we are in a delightful dream, or in a nightmare, or in alternating REM episodes of pleasure and pain, courage and fear, success and failure, acceptance and rejection, strength and weakness, fame and ignominy, and so forth through all the ups and downs of this creaky, unstable, and unsturdy see-saw of existence, that to awaken will be to die. Therefore, we continue in our dream as the only consciousness of which we are sure.

Many have suggested that this present existence we find ourselves participating in is but a preparation for, and far inferior to, an existence we will live elsewhere after death. Often, the same thinkers suggest that this "afterlife" will be better only for those who are members of certain groups, or who have behaved correctly, or who have thought correctly, or who have had the good fortune to have made everything "right" at the last moment. For the others, which usually includes the majority of humankind, they believe the afterlife will be literally *hell.* But most of us have not had the chance, like Lazarus, to investigate the validity of this claim. Certainly, *it takes no effort to imagine a better existence and just as little effort to imagine a worse one.* However, circumstantial evidence would suggest that many people only give "lip service" to this possibility. These "lip-service" people may include most "after-life" proponents who cry at funerals. They don't cry because they believe the deceased has gone to the infernal regions, and they certainly don't cry because they believe the deceased has achieved an improved state of being; they cry because the deceased is *dead.* They may also cry because the event presents them with inescapable proof that they too must leave the land of the living some day.

Others have claimed that our "souls," which they define as our metaphysical, spiritual essences, transmigrate through the ages from creature to creature, and then from human being to human being,

9

finally reaching their penultimate "home" in a very holy person, and their ultimate "home" in achieving Nirvana, a state of not needing to return to any earthly existence unless we wish to do so in order to help others. This hypothesis, as the "afterlife" one previously presented, assumes that we do, indeed, have "souls." This is itself a controversial point for some, although most would assent to belief in the existence of what is usually called "the human spirit," and many have an uncanny feeling that they are living in their bodies as observers. Furthermore, there is possible evidence of the validity of the "transmigration" theory in the often repeated experience of having met strangers we feel upon first meeting we have known "all our lives" (the phrase can be read both ways).

In brief, there is very possibly much more to what we call "life" than most of us realize, and many ways of perceiving it, some of which, or most of which, may be true.

Yet, many people are not wholeheartedly willing to entertain most of this "more" or many of these "ways," for there persists within them a gut-level intuition that existence starts with birth and ends with death—and that all theories that suggest otherwise are but wishful thinking. Theologians have always had misgivings about such a seemingly bleak outlook, for they have always been concerned that without the hope of future reward or fear of future punishment beyond our present existence, we would behave without scruples, without conscience, and without anxiety about consequences. Yet, as everyone either knows, or has learned, or is learning the hard way, *there is no such thing as a sane, intelligent, informed person acting without scruples or without conscience.* Normal human beings are simply not "built" that way. And just as surely, *there is no such thing as anyone acting without consequences,* give or take some extreme pathological exceptions. Suppress "guilt" with your mind, and it will pop up later in your gall bladder, and on the way there in self-punishing behavior. Our comeuppance awaits for us right here and now and/or here and later in this life, despite what may sometimes appear as miscarriages of universal justice. Perhaps we have read our religious metaphors incorrectly. Even if there is no "afterlife," theologians don't have to worry about the loss of reward and retribution. That kind of R. and R., especially at the psychosomatic level, will always be with us.

****

Whatever you believe life is, I would suggest that to make the best you can of the amazing experience called your present lifetime right here on planet earth is to make it exciting and rewarding for both yourself and others. So, if it is a movie, make it an outstanding, award-winning one. If you are nothing more than a collection of vibrations, make those vibrations harmonize, make your life a well-composed symphony. If life is a dream, learn the techniques of lucid dreaming, and be "awake" in your dream so that you can arrange it as a dream you can recollect with satisfaction. If there is life after death, don't negate the one before—don't forget to live life *before* death! If you are living just one of many lifetimes, apply some of the lessons you learned the last times around to making this one better. And whether life is only a one-time happening, or any permutation or combination of the many possibilities that people have proposed, *celebrate its joys, deal bravely with its challenges, and make it a positive, life-giving, life-sharing experience for yourself and all those whose lives you touch.*

Whatever you believe life is, "give it your best shot." Don't waste it. Don't degrade it. Don't destroy it. We, and the generations to follow us, are all in this together, and nobody, as the saying goes, is getting out alive. Meanwhile, *let us help one another truly be alive.*

In the space-time continuum (whether it be actual or illusory) within which we all have our present existence, *let us live life, not die through it.*

And what does it mean to live life?

It means, as I have suggested, to make the most of it, to make of it something you can look back at with humble pride, something that has truly enriched you and others in the most important ways.

It means not sleeping your life away, not spending too much of your precious time in a state of passive and vicarious living, not devoting excessive time to escaping those aspects of reality that you and I are responsible for.

It means developing your capabilities, all your spiritual (however you interpret the term), mental, emotional, and physical potentials, so that your life is worthwhile to you and a benefit to others.

It means getting yourself in shape and keeping yourself fit at every level of your potential. It means making of yourself the kind of person both *you and others* can enjoy being with.

*It means participating actively and enthusiastically and gratefully in the main event of your life—YOUR LIFE!*

It's your life, but it's also part of mine, and part of all those who have lived, are living, and will live. And *you owe it to yourself and to all of us to be the best you can be, to make the most out of your life that you can, to contribute your part to making our mutually shared experience a good one.*

Life is not a "freebie."

Life is an awesome and wonderful responsibility.

*Live it!*

Live it with style, with grace.

Live it successfully, even in your failures.

This is your time to "[strut] upon the stage." Don't leave us with "a tale told by an idiot…signifying nothing." When you make your exit, make it having given us a reason to applaud.

You might even get called back for an encore you didn't expect.

# MY GOOD FRIEND, DEATH

> *"...if we do not learn to perceive the mystery and beauty of our present life, our present hour, we shall not perceive the worth of any life, of any hour."*
>
> —*Huston Smith*

We love to personify everything. Opportunity is a wealthy traveler who sometimes knocks at our door. Luck is a capricious lady who sometimes smiles at us or at other times ignores us. And Time is an impatient, old, grandfatherly codger who cantankerously refuses to wait for us.

Most interestingly of all, we have even given life to life's so-called opposite—Death. For, though most of us would like to deny the fact, Death is still, as he was in medieval times, the grim reaper who can arrive when we least expect him, the proud and mighty ruler of a vast domain, the grinning skeleton waiting to take our hand in the "*danse macabre*," the pale rider on a pale horse who eventually seeks us out and claims us all—with the cooperation of those other necessary personifications: Opportunity, Luck, and Time.

But why give Death life? It seems very generous of us. Or is it only fair? Isn't the exchange a simple *quid pro quo?* For doesn't Death give us life also?

Death remembered, after all, *encourages* us to make more out of life (that is, unless we are cowards; in which case, we aren't making much out of life

14

anyhow), *encourages* us "to love that well which [we]…must leave ere long," to borrow once more from the highly quotable bard of Stratford-on-Avon.

Death forgotten, on the other hand, lulls us into making less of life, for we begin to think of our present existence as a permanent possession, rather than as the temporary loan that it is.

If you are willing to adapt a realistic view of life, one that includes Death, and one ironically that can be the opposite of morbid, Death can be your friend every day; for Death will say to you, "Look, my friend, you have yet another day of life, another possibility of another twenty-four hours of borrowed time, another bestowal of the incredible gift of life."

Perhaps you have not been fortunate enough to meet Death and almost leave life in his company as I did at the age of thirteen. On the way to class, I misjudged where to place my right hand on a door with three large, horizontal glass panels that was swinging shut toward me. Instead of catching the door on its wooden frame above the handle and reversing its momentum, I heard a terrible crash and in disbelief watched my forearm go through the glass pane next to the frame. When I instinctively pulled my arm back, my wrist was ripped open by a jagged, upright piece of glass that looked very much like a dagger—and had the same brutal effect. I turned to the student behind me, and as I showed him my arm, the blood from the main artery in my wrist spurted up into his face. The school nurse arrived shortly, and, after she gave me first aid, I was rushed to the hospital. Had the teacher driving gotten there five minutes later than he did, I would have been "dead on arrival."

When I awoke from my emergency operation, I was a different person. I have rarely since taken life for granted. The scar on my right wrist remains to this day as my constant *memento mori,* serving the same purpose as the human skull or hourglass on the study desk did for scholars of an earlier time. I am almost always amazed when I get up in the morning and discover that the mountains, the trees, our lawn, and our driveway are still there, that I am still around to experience life once more for another day, or whatever portion of it I will be able to enjoy. Of course, some days I forget. On those days, I just go through the motions, I just do my imitation of "being alive." And, oh yes, I do have a problem with the expression, "I'll see you later." I know full well that it could be a lie. One of the parties involved might not be available again. Strangely enough, lots of people have no such doubts.

I have known others who have had the same good fortune, others who by meeting Death have learned to love life. We all recognize each other immediately, for we all see in each other the same daily gratitude for and appreciation of the wonder of life. Thanks to Death, we live full lives, rarely taking a day for granted.

If you haven't had the benefit of a similar experience, I would recommend that you see or read Thorton Wilder's play, *Our Town.* After the young ingenue, Emily Webb, dies in childbirth, she is able, through the magic of the theater, to visit earth and relive her sixteenth birthday. However, she quickly comes to realize that nobody—neither her mother, nor her father, nor anyone she tries to communicate with upon her return—understands how precious life is, for everyone is treating life as a relatively empty and ordinary routine. People are not really listening to each other. People are not really paying attention to each other. People hardly seem to notice the beauty of nature. They seem completely unaware of the miracle of their own or anybody's existence. Their self-imposed loneliness, their self-chosen alienation from each other and from all that surrounds them, fills her with overwhelming sadness and dismay. Of her own volition she ends her "experiment" within minutes. It is too painful to witness. She cannot "relive" that which no one, including herself, actually "lived."

When you wake up tomorrow morning and see or hear that the world is still outside your window, think twice. For you, for me, for anyone, it doesn't have to be there. Death can show up any time. Until he does, shrouded in his black monk's robe, as in Ingmar Bergman's classic movie about the Black Plague, *The Seventh Seal,* or attired as Emily Dickinson's perfect Nineteenth-Century suitor, in her poem, "Because I Could Not Stop For Death," *today is another day of whatever number of days you have been allotted by Opportunity, Luck, and Time.*

*Carpe Diem.* Make the day meaningful and rewarding for yourself and others. Share your love of life while you have the opportunity, luck, and time to do so.

*Carpe Diem.* Not everyone who begins the day will end it. Treat others as if you won't see them again. You might not. I recall a student telling me about how she still regrets having had a very unpleasant and unnecessary argument with her uncle, an argument that left him feeling unloved and unappreciated, an argument that was never resolved because he was killed in a car accident twenty minutes later on his way home.

> *Carpe Diem.*
> Once the day is gone,
> it will not return.

*Procrastinate any trivial thing you wish, but don't procrastinate your involvement in life.*

Don't procrastinate enjoyment, affection, sharing, or helping.

Don't procrastinate encouraging yourself and others to participate fully in the present.

> *Carpe Diem.*
> Thank Death for teaching you its value.
> Spend it wisely.

> *Seize the Day.*
> Horace is dead.
> You are alive.

## THE GIFT

YOUR LIFE
IS A GIFT:

ENJOY IT;

USE IT
WELL;

SHARE IT
GLADLY;

RETURN IT
WITHOUT REGRET.

*Clay Boland Jr.*

# SECTION II: THE QUESTION

*Clay Boland Jr.*

# WHAT ARE YOU DOING HERE?

> *"Most of us do not...[take the] time to sit down and work out...what life is all about.... But the danger then is that life becomes purposeless, haphazard and dreary."*
> —John Foster Dulles

> *"What most people want—young or old—is not merely security, or comfort, or luxury, although they are glad enough to have these. Most of all, they want meaning in their lives."*
> —from the Rockefeller Report on Education, 1958

Often the simplest questions are the hardest ones to answer. The basics of human existence can be more complex than the intricacies of quantum physics. Finding a sound major premise to build your life on can be harder than creating sophisticated and logically valid syllogistic arguments in order to deductively derive the many "conclusions" from your premise that you need to guide you through the various and constantly changing problems of life.

Take, for example, the old syllogistic textbook "chestnut" about John and his mortality. A diagram of the syllogism would look something like this:

| MAJOR PREMISE: | All people<br>*(Middle Term)* | are mortal.<br>*(Predicate)* |
| --- | --- | --- |
| MINOR PREMISE: | John<br>*(Subject)* | is a person.<br>*(Middle Term)* |
| CONCLUSION: | John<br>*(Subject)* | is mortal.<br>*(Predicate)* |

The *major premise* of this syllogism is that "All people are mortal."

The *minor premise* is that "John is a person." Proceeding by the rules of syllogistic logic, you can test the legitimacy of the "middle term," which is "All people" in the major premise and "a person" in the minor premise.

Within the group called "All people" would be included each individual "person." Therefore, you can propose that the middle term has no "distribution" problems. In other cases, such as a major premise that starts with "Some people" or a major premise that is too vague, there are further logical problems to deal with before you can say that the first two statements of your syllogism can be *validly* connected; i.e., correctly connected by the laws of pure logic (laws which operate independently of and have nothing to do with the soundness; i.e., the truth, of your statements).

Once you have established the connection, you can discard the middle term, which has served its purpose, unite the remaining "half" statements, by putting the first half of the minor premise with the second half of the major premise, and conclude that "John is mortal."

Sounds difficult, doesn't it? Actually, with a little practice it becomes easier.

What appears at first to be easy, *finding an acceptable major premise,* which in this case is that "All people are mortal," *is much more difficult,* for it soon becomes apparent that there are a number of differing opinions as to the soundness of this major premise and of almost any other one you can think of to use in creating a syllogism for a deductive argument. In this case, some will be of the opinion that the statement is true. But just as many will claim that it isn't, that "All people are *immortal,"* that although their bodies die, the "spirit" or "soul" that animates them never does.

And so it is with finding a major premise in answer to the fundamental question, "What are you doing here?" The task is not an easy one. But *whatever your answer is, it will be the major premise by which you live your life.* In most cases, it will be what is known as a "working" hypothesis, one that you believe "works," one that you perceive to be "sound," and one that can serve you until you find a better one—if a better one presents itself. If you are lucky, it will be a life-centering rather than a life-disorienting hypothesis, for a sound "working" hypothesis can serve as a reliable map to help you find your way through the journey of life; whereas an unsound "working" hypothesis, or no "working" hypothesis at all, can leave you wandering and lost in a dark and perplexing Daedelean labyrinth, with the Minotaur of anomie waiting for you around every corner.

This is not to suggest that you need to leap from the cradle muttering the magic mantra that is the answer to the riddle of your existence. It is, however, to suggest that as a true student of life you will *continue to search for the answer, readjust your life— if need be—as you do, and organize your priorities and goals to help you live your answer to this question.*

Your answer, or "working" hypothesis, may change as your investigation proceeds. You may even find a good answer, reject it, and return to it later. Or your answer may remain constant throughout your life once you have discovered it. Whatever the vicissitudes of your own, unique, individual search may be, the important thing to remember is to give continuous and serious thought to the question and to live, in as far as it is possible, by what you have carefully considered to be the best and most sound answer, or major premise, that you are able to find.

Ask some of your friends, "What are you doing here?" You'll be surprised how many answer, "I don't know," or "I haven't really thought much about it." Or you'll justifiably be concerned when others answer with superficial and/or shortsighted statements for their major "working" hypothesis such as, "I'm here to make money," or "I'm here to party." Amazingly enough, there are lots of people who will *never* give the question more thought than demonstrated by these four "typical" answers. As a result, they will go through life creating unnecessary dissatisfaction, frustration, and difficulties for themselves and others. Of course, they can get lucky and have circumstances answer the question for them. This happens for many through parenthood and/or fortuitous career choices.

Nevertheless, there are some poor "lost souls" who at the end of almost a century of living still have very little idea of what they *were* or *are* doing here. Among these are some otherwise very intelligent people who can identify every tree in the forest but have very little idea what the forest looks like from the mountain top, since they have not thought it worthwhile, or thought it too time-consuming and difficult, to climb up there to look at the "bigger picture."

And yet a number of good answers have always been and still are available, despite the fact that they are harder to find and to "follow" for us who live in these perplexing modern times than they were for our less-technologically-advanced-but-more-value-oriented ancestors.

The answers are *available* through all education (religious and secular), communicative arts, and personal experience bringing us in contact with the basic issues of life and how to live it. Components and guidelines for shaping your answer can be found, for instance, in many time-honored, well-loved works of art, music, and literature—in Rembrandt's magnificent series of self-portraits that he painted from his youth to his old age, which tell us "Live life with compassion"; in Beethoven's *Fifth Symphony,* which repeats one resounding message from start to finish "Live life with courage '•••—!'"; and in Hemingway's short novel, *The Old Man and the Sea,* which suggests that we live our lives with both; i.e., with both compassion and courage—and with dignity and integrity as well.

The answers can be *avoided* through all education (religious and secular), communicative arts, and personal experience devoted to distracting and/or insulating us from the basic issues of life and how to live it. Vestigial religious dietary laws, for example,

27

focus their adherents' attention on nonessential issues and thus distract their attention from the more central, ethical answers given by their particular belief system to the question, "What are you doing here?"

And, of course, answers can be found—and avoided—through your own observing, thinking, and meditating; as well as through your own intuitions and emotions, and through your conversations with others.

As you can readily see, *THIS QUESTION IS THE QUINTESSENTIAL EXISTENTIAL QUESTION. IT IS THE QUESTION OF WHAT IT IS THAT GIVES YOUR LIFE ITS CENTRAL PURPOSE, ITS CENTRAL MEANING.*

Various religions and philosophies have dealt with the question and have given answers that have satisfied millions of people from all walks of life and of all degrees of intelligence. And, in the past, religious organizations, educational institutions, and families have passed these answers on to each new generation.

But in modern times the spiritual, intellectual, and moral influence of religion, education, and family has declined drastically. Moreover, modern humankind—seemingly having broken with not only a number of the worst aspects of the past but with also a number of the best—having, so to speak, "thrown out the baby with the bath water"—now, through every new individual, has to "reinvent the wheel."

Religious movements, nationalistic movements, and political "belief" systems are some of the "varieties of group existentialism" (to paraphrase William James) giving their followers a "central meaning," even if this, in many instances, engenders a fanaticism often repugnant and sometimes even fatal to other members of the human race.

Individual philosophies, such as those presented in the works of Sartre and Camus (the two best-known writers of the modern "existentialism" movement), are more common today in the more "advanced" parts of the world. These are philosophies which individuals shape for themselves and then shape their lives around, with courage and commitment, in order to create purpose and meaning for their existences, even though a number of these also are sometimes more harmful than helpful to the rest of us.

However, there is no need to reject, in forming an individual philosophy, the wisdom of endless generations who have lived before you. As a matter of fact, incorporating the best of the "tried and true" wisdom of the past in your own individual philosophy will probably help guide and direct you in developing a sound philosophical answer to the question, "What are you doing here?"

If your answer to this question is too *self-centered,* you are more than likely setting yourself up for a very lonely and empty life no matter how many friends and acquaintances you will claim you have. We are born as individuals but also as members of a larger group of individuals; and, whatever your answer is, it should show that you have included other people in your philosophy.

If your answer to this question is too *altruistic,* you are no doubt asking for a lot of hurt feelings and disappointments. To set yourself up as a cosmic "doormat" is to invite one and all to wipe their feet on you and step on you. Extend your charity and support to yourself, for you'll need both to sustain yourself through the efforts and defeats involved in extending them to others.

Somewhere in between the polarities of an overly self-centered answer and an overly altruistic answer is an answer that will satisfy both yourself and others.

If it's a mature, intelligent one, it will give your life a mature, intelligent purpose and meaning—a purpose and meaning that you will find to be constantly rewarding.

If it's a challenging one, it will make your life challenging—for it will make it imperative that you develop the strength of character needed to maintain the dedication it calls for.

And, despite your best intentions, as I have learned time and again in teaching many different courses, if what you think is happening according to your "syllabus" is not the "main event" that you are creating for others, be ready to realize that *your intellectual answer to the question may not be the same as your behavioral answer.* Your behavioral answer may be better; it may be worse. Therefore, you'll need to be flexible enough to adjust in the right direction. When I first taught "Principles of Speech," I thought I was teaching oratory. When I discovered that the main thing I was teaching and the main subject the students were learning was "self-confidence," I redesigned my syllabus to deal with both subjects.

College courses, I might add, bring to mind an excellent analogy for living life with or without an important purpose or central meaning. For what could be worse than a course with content of dubious importance in which you never have any idea as to what is going on, why it's going on, or why you are taking the course at all? And what could be better than one that sets out to teach you something you know *is* important, that gives you definitive guidelines, and that you finish with that good feeling of knowing that the experience was worthwhile?

Search for your answer, test the validity of your answer, develop and "live" it into a good answer for both yourself and others.

Make it work, readjusting it or changing it as necessary.

Replace it with a better one, if you find a better one.

All the study, all the work, all the "revisions," you put into this independent "research" and "experiential" project will be worth it. For the course you are taking is *your life*.

And the grade you will get for the course will be one, in the final analysis, that you yourself will assign yourself when the course is over.

When you find the best answer, you will probably never have to readjust it or change it again.

It will see you
> through "sickness and health,"
> through pain and pleasure,
> through bad times and good times,
> through being young and being old,
> through living and dying—

with MEANING,

with PURPOSE,

with a feeling of ACCOMPLISHMENT.

# SECTION III: SOME OBSERVATIONS

*Clay Boland Jr.*

## BEING HUMAN

To be human is to be both good and bad, to be both courageous and cowardly, to be both kind and cruel, to be both agreeable and disagreeable, to be both cooperative and stubborn, to be both considerate and rude, to be both honest and deceitful, to be both loving and malevolent, to be both generous and stingy, to be both altruistic and selfish, to be both helpful and hindering, to be both caring and indifferent, to be both sensible and irrational, to be both platonic and sensual, to be both virtuous and vicious.

We all contain within us Sophocles' indomitable Antigone *and* her spineless sister, Ismene; Robert Louis Stevenson's respectable Dr. Jekyll *and* his alter ego, the fiendish Mr. Hyde; Jonathan Swift's rational Houyhnhnmn *and* bestial Yahoo; Abraham Maslow's "self-actualizing," healthy individual and M. Scott Peck's "self-deceiving," sick individual portrayed in his *People of the Lie;* the kindly, little-known Max Ehrmann, creator of the "Desiderata," *and the* cruel, notorious Marquis de Sade; the charitable Mother Teresa of modern-day India *and* the murderous Lucretia Borgia of Renaissance Italy. These "symbolic" representations of human potential are themselves only partial representations, for they are known only for one particular trait—and nobody can be reduced to a single trait.

To pretend that to be human is either the first or the second of these *seeming* opposites is to believe in an illusion, the illusion of an ersatz, non-existent creature—the dichotomized human. For *within each one of us is a unique synthesis of what it means to be human.* And to be human is not an "either-or" affair; it is a "both-and" struggle.

To pretend that the human condition is either side of the dichotomy is to court disaster. And yet too many of our personal histories and too much of the history of our world can be seen as that very disaster courted and "won" in millions of Pyrrhic victories by those suffering from the deleterious effects of dichotomized thinking and living.

To try to live as if either side of the dichotomy were the true human condition is to court disaster because *it is impossible to be half a human.*

Take, for instance, the more common extreme of living as if only the first half of the dichotomy were true. You can manage the self-deception and the deception of others outrageously successfully for long periods of time. You may even actually come to believe yourself to be a magnificent tightrope artist who no longer has any need for the safety nets of life available to ordinary mortals. Nonetheless, your "act" eventually catches up with you, and when you fall, if others see you or get in the way, they, as well as you yourself, are hurt. And whether anyone sees you or not, the injuries sustained bring you quickly back to the reality of your situation. Despite all this, you will probably be anxious to get right back on the rope and try again to desperately teeter-totter through life, unbalanced. This is not to say that you should not try to be better than you are, but to suggest that you should not try to be something that has no resemblance to a complete, genuine human being.

Living by the other half of the dichotomy is no better in its effects on the individual. Moreover, it is usually a lot worse in its effects on others. For no one is either totally noble or totally ignoble, despite what the fabricators of cowboy movies, police and detective dramas, and murder thrillers, or even the war propagandists, would have us believe. To conclude that your worst possible tendencies or actions should be the norm for yourself and everyone else is to reach a very hasty generalization based on insufficient evidence. Such a conclusion would more than likely be based on your own personal convenience rather than on a more objective and honest appraisal. As with your opposite, your fellow extremist, you can deceive yourself and others fairly easily—after all, the line of least resistance is an easy line to represent. But in time, you will discover that you have sold yourself and all your customers a "bill of bads," and you'll feel lower than Arthur Miller's bewildered salesman, Willie Loman, ever felt, for you will have truly cheated on your better half.

Folk symbolism has dismissed this latter group, the deniers of the reality of their better halves, with various bestial labels such as "pig," "goat," "weasel," "shark," "wolf," "ape," or simply, "animal." The symbolism at least keeps this prodigal group among the living. After all, humans can understand those who "err." But far greater verbal scorn is reserved for the former group, those who deny the reality of their worse halves. They are described with epithets of stiffness, sternness, graveness, and other terms more fitting for the dead than the quick. One of the popular terms used at present to describe such people is "up-tight," but one of the oldest and best images, because intentionally meant to be both shocking and scandalous, is their being graphically pictured as having broomsticks strategically planted in their posteriors. After all, to act "divine" is damn near unforgivable and as unnatural as the image suggests.

Neither group of extremists deals with the reality of the human condition. Both groups eventually become victims of their own misguided judgments. Both eventually suffer the inevitable and painful backlash that results from pretending to be only half human.

Furthermore, the person who *pretends* to be a saint and the person who *pretends* to be a sinner are both hypocrites. Neither offers us an example worth following. But we can thank them both for offering us excellent lessons on how *not* to live.

Nonetheless, many of us often find ourselves inclined to be extremists and to encourage others to join us, for *we find it difficult to accept ourselves and others as fully human, despite the fact that all the evidence we will ever need to return the correct verdict is within us. We ourselves are the best and most conclusive proof of our own innocence and guilt, of our own potential for better or for worse that only awaits the proper or improper circumstances to be put into action.*

You might claim that you would never rob a bank and cannot understand why anyone else would do so. But if you were poor enough and desperate enough, you yourself might be there, wearing a bandanna to cover your nose and mouth, and shaking in your shoes, hoping not to have to use the gun in your hand, and already thinking about spending the best part of your life in jail if your "plan" fails.

*All* of the tendencies, *all* the potential behaviors, and *all* the good and bad that humans are capable of performing find expression in one way or another in your life. In that sense, you are no better or worse than anyone else, living or dead, even though you may be less famous or more fortunate. You might never be an internationally known leader in the struggle for justice, but you may win a number of significant and difficult struggles against your own selfishness in trying to be fair to others in your personal life. You might not make intellectual or philanthropic contributions to world peace, but you may encourage joy and caring in your family and community. On the other hand, you may never feel the need to rob a bank, as in the example given earlier, but find yourself sorely tempted to steal someone else's spouse. Or you might never lob a mortar shell at your neighbors but only tarnish their reputations with gossip.

The most basic truths about ourselves and all other "selves" are literally self-evident. And yet, we refuse to believe our eyes, our hearts, or any of our other excellent "witnesses." We find these truths so hard to take that we prefer to believe lies. They are more flattering. And therefore, they are more popular.

But the unavoidable, irrefutable fact is—WE ARE HUMAN. And to be human is (to borrow Henry James' comment on being an American) a "complex fate." Being human does not offer us the stark simplicity, limited possibilities, and premature *rigor mortis* or primordial bestiality of "either-or," but the rich complexity, myriad possibilities, and lifelong "aliveness" of "both-and."

And the problem of accepting this is not that we become "disillusioned" with ourselves and with others, but that we allow ourselves and encourage others, and others allow themselves and encourage others, ourselves included, to be "illusioned" in the first place.

The result of eventually "learning the truth" about ourselves and others is often a pendulum swing from admiration to loathing, from trying to emulate the best in others to giving up and practicing the worst in others, from having faith in human potential to becoming apostates who have decided that humankind is hopeless.

But neither being "illusioned" nor being "disillusioned" is healthy since neither state is based on the reality of the human condition. The one derives from our propensity to hope, as well as from our desire to "look good" and to see those around us as better than they are; the other from our willingness to despair, and from our disbelief when we discover others are not innately different or significantly better than we are.

When the pendulum, having gradually moved back and forth less and less, finally settles in a middle, balanced position, we see *beyond illusion and disillusion to the reality of the full range of humanity in each and every one of us.*

And when that happens, and *only then, can we learn to accept ourselves and others.*

*"Know yourself,"* as the ancient saying advises, *and you know what it means to be human.* And considering the evidence, rather than being

"illusioned" or "disillusioned," be glad that we all have done as well as we have.

ALTHOUGH WE ALL POSSESS
THE POTENTIAL TO BE A LOT
BETTER THAN WE ARE,
WE ALSO ALL POSSESS
THE POTENTIAL TO BE
A WHOLE LOT
WORSE THAN WE ARE.

And so do you.

And so do I.

# THE HUMAN SPIRIT

Winston Smith is a minority of one who defies the nightmare, totalitarian world depicted by George Orwell in his novel, *1984.* After his inevitable capture, imprisonment, and torture, Winston tells O'Brien, a powerful inner-party agent for Big Brother, that the government of Oceania will eventually fall, for it will never defeat the human spirit. O'Brien laughs cynically and props the emaciated Winston in front of a three-panel mirror, as if to say, *"This* is what will overcome the 'boot-in-the-face' tactics of a powerful, all-pervasive totalitarianism? Ha!"

Our hero sees before him in the mirror a shriveled bag of skin and bones covered with ugly bruises and sores. His face hardly conceals the bony Yorick skull beneath. He gasps. He certainly does appear to be a pitiful and ridiculous embodiment of the human spirit. And yet, it takes constant surveillance, repression of every aspect of his life, and highly sophisticated torture and brainwashing to finally bring Winston, before the novel ends, to succumb, to bring him to love Big Brother. *The human spirit does not surrender readily.*

A young high-school athlete, who lived in a small town in Western Colorado, lost his left arm when he was fourteen years old due to the presence of bone cancer. The arm was amputated in an attempt to arrest the spread of this cancer. Despite the loss, this young athlete eventually managed not only to play varsity basketball and baseball, but to play them more effectively than most two-armed players. Indeed, he was more than effective, he was a star. He was also a great inspiration.

By the time he was seventeen, the cancer appeared in his shoulder and elsewhere. It became obvious that he would never survive to celebrate his eighteenth birthday. Nevertheless, he continued his athletic career as long as possible—and even during his terminal hospitalization never lost his fortitude. *The human spirit is not defeated easily.*

Endless photographs reaffirm the power of the human spirit. The following three come to mind: six World War II United States marines raising the American flag in the midst of intense gunfire on the summit of Mount Suribachi on Iwo Jima in 1945; a handful of unarmed students bravely challenging Soviet tanks in the otherwise unusually deserted streets of Budapest in the 1956 Hungarian uprising against communist suppression; and thousands of young Chinese men and women staging a demonstration for freedom in Beijing's Tiananmen Square in 1989, a demonstration they must have known could not be countenanced by a government fearful of losing totalitarian control over a fifth of the world's population. *The human spirit defies death itself.*

And what is this human spirit? Is it tangible? Not really. Does that mean that it doesn't exist? No.

Philosophers and theologians have defined it, or tried. Scientists are baffled by it, and they therefore attempt to dismiss it—theoretically—but find it embarrassingly present in their own lives. The important thing is that *it exists.*

It is the force within us that motivates our nobler actions, our selfless sacrifices, and our greatest works of art, music, literature, theater, and thought.

It is the force within us that many believe makes us immortal. Certainly, at the very least, it makes our species "immortal." For since the human spirit does not die but continues from generation to generation, it gives our species a "spiritual immortality." It is our species' soul.

The human spirit is our "special" heritage. It is part of every human life. We feel it stir within us when we practice love for our neighbors, when we overcome great obstacles in achieving personal victories, when we forget our petty concerns in serving greater causes, when we put our convenience or security, our reputations, our incomes, or even our lives on the line for the principles of justice, equality, and liberty.

The human spirit has been omnipresent throughout the ages in all people, in all places.

*The human spirit is not the exclusive property of any racial, ethnic, national, age, geographical, economic, political, social, religious or non-religious, well-educated or poorly educated, masculine or feminine group. It is the heritage of every single human being who has ever lived, is living, or will live.*

It is the one thing we all have in common.

But, unfortunately, it is more common for the majority of us to suppress it than to express it.

And since we are the species least victimized by instinct and most able to learn by education, *we must insure that we instill respect for the human spirit as the most central part of every generation's education.* For what is the most essential thing we all need to learn and develop? What is the basic subject that we cannot relegate to secondary importance without grievous consequences for individuals everywhere and for society, both local and global? What but the cultivation of the human spirit! Education and culture without this are lifeless, are meaningless, are robotic, are impersonal, and are literally deadly.

*The human spirit is our greatest possession.*

*It is also our greatest responsibility.*

Neglect or ignore it in yourself and in others, and we all wither.

Nurture and learn from it in yourself and in others, and we all flourish.

# YOUR HERITAGE

Take a trip to a museum of natural history in a large city and go to the section on the development of humankind. Study the exhibits showing the thousands and thousands of years of humankind's struggle for survival. Look at the reproductions of the Lascaux cave paintings depicting animals our ancestors hunted in 15,000 B.C. Picture yourself as the artist creating these lifelike paintings by the dim light of a crude wick burning in a small, hollowed-out stone filled with animal fat, or picture yourself hunting the most behemothic of these wild beasts using as your only weapon a wooden spear tipped with a large flint arrowhead.

Take a trip to an art museum in a large city and go to the exhibits of the art of ancient cultures. Try to imagine playing an ancient Sumerian "harp" or drinking from an ornate Assyrian wine cup made of gold. Look at the artistic remains and remnants of the Babylonian, Egyptian, Cretan, Grecian, and Roman empires.

Move into the rooms housing artifacts from the European Middle Ages. Try to imagine yourself as a devout worshipper inspired by the stained-glass windows from some old cathedral, or imagine yourself wearing the armor suit of a knight, or watching a jousting match in Camelot.

Proceed to the Renaissance exhibit and wonder at the magnificence of the sculpture and delight in the newly discovered use of perspective in the paintings of the time. Look carefully at the beautifully rendered portraits of lords and ladies and high-ranking members of the clergy. Try to study their characters—their strengths and weaknesses.

Continue through the Baroque rooms, the Age of Revolution rooms, the Industrial Age rooms, and the Modern Age rooms.

Move into the rooms housing similar examples of the evolution of culture in the Far East, in Africa, in India, and on the continents that Columbus mistook for India, the Americas.

Or read about the story of humankind in books, or study it through documentaries shown on television, such as Ken Burns' excellent "recounting" of the Civil War that was made for the Public Broadcasting System, mainly from old Civil War photographs, letters, and newspaper stories.

Take courses in World Culture. Learn about a culture completely "foreign" to you. And, also, get to know the art, music, literature, and history of your own culture—from its beginning, not just from your "date of birth."

Travel, if you can, and see the actual places mentioned and shown in your books or on television: the buildings that have housed the great figures of history, the rivers and seas that invited the great explorers, and the fields where large armies met and fought, and where many died, often for what they hoped would be a better future for others.

Get to know your heritage.

*Your generation has received the benefits of the efforts, sacrifices, discoveries, inventions, and ideas of people striving and struggling through innumerable centuries.* These people have often made mistakes. But if enough members of your generation know about their mistakes, there's a chance your generation will not have to repeat them.

*Throughout the ages, people have thought about the important issues of life and have recorded their findings in books, in plays, in paintings, in statues, in architecture, in music, in dance, and in poems.* All of this is also part of the inheritance of your generation. They were often wrong in their views, but just as often they were extremely accurate in their insights. There is much to be learned from them.

*The story of humankind does not have as its framework one ethnic, racial, or social group in one small part of one particular country on one particular continent during the lifetime of one or two generations believing in one or two particular sets of values, or not believing in any set of values.*

The story of humankind is rich and varied.

It is full of treasures for those who wish to look for them.

Don't impoverish yourself by only allowing yourself a narrow, provincial view of human existence. We are no longer living in the Dark Ages when most people rarely traveled more than fourteen miles from their native village, could not read, had very little education, and knew almost nothing about history, politics, other cultures, and other people.

Know what others have labored throughout the world and throughout the centuries to create.

KNOW YOUR HERITAGE.

## "HUMANUNKIND"

The American poet and artist, e. e. cummings, who preferred lower-case letters for the expression of his higher thoughts, coined the word "manunkind" to depict our species' infliction of perpetual grief and suffering on its own members. If he were writing today, he would have probably used the more inclusive-sounding term, "humanunkind." Either way, it's hard to brush aside the accusation. We stand condemned. *All of us.*

Except for an occasional misanthrope, misogynist, cynic, or "madperson," I have never met anyone who approves of or applauds the sad testaments given by our history books, documentaries, and daily news reports of our cruelty to each other, of humankind's inhumanity to humankind. Rather, most people are horrified and depressed by the endless slaughter, brutality, exploitation, indignities, and inequities of which so many of the inhabitants of this globe have been and still are the victims.

I doubt that we will ever more than partially remove these gross violations of human rights from the story of humankind. I do believe, however, that we can improve the situation through political and individual action. I will leave discussion of solving the problems by involvement in political organizations to those more qualified to do so. On the individual level, and in our daily lives, however, I would propose that we all can alleviate the situation by being aware that our own individual minor "unkindnesses" to others are the "germ seeds" of the major "humanunkindnesses" recorded in history, in documentaries, and in the news media. Even the mightiest oak starts as a small and seemingly insignificant acorn.

Therefore, when we criticize *the world's "unkindnesses,"* we need also to recognize that they are *extensions and enlargements of our own "unkindnesses."* They are our own, perhaps not in severity, but in type. In that sense, we are to blame also.

Here are what I perceive as some of the *causes* of humanity's inhumanity to humanity. They are *beliefs, fears,* and *failures* which I would suggest can be lessened in our individual treatment of our fellow human beings:

BELIEVING THAT OTHERS
ARE LESS HUMAN
THAN WE ARE;

BELIEVING THAT OUR PARTICULAR
THOUGHT SYSTEM IS SUPERIOR
TO THAT OF OTHERS;

BELIEVING THAT IT IS IMPERATIVE
**NOT** TO FORGIVE "THOSE WHO
TRESPASS AGAINST US";

FEARING **NOT** TO BELIEVE
WHATEVER OUR PEERS OR
THE AUTHORITIES BELIEVE;

FEARING TO DEFEND WHAT IS JUST
IF WE FEEL IT IS TOO COSTLY
FOR US TO DEFEND IT;

FAILING TO RECOGNIZE OUR OWN
COMPLICITY IN WHAT HAPPENS
IN THE WORLD; AND

FAILING TO PRACTICE EMPATHY
IN OUR DEALINGS
WITH EACH OTHER.

I'm sure you can think of some more causes such as GREED, INDIFFERENCE, and that old nemesis of humanity, IGNORANCE.

Whatever you add to the list, the point is to realize, along with Pogo, that "We have met the enemy and they are us." Therefore *it is up to each one of us in our own lives to individually initiate a personal crusade against humankind's inhumanity to humankind.*

The alternative is to sit back and do nothing while we "let George do it."

But to do nothing is to play right back into the hands of the misanthropes, misogynists, cynics, and "madpersons" of this world, and into the hands of a small number of well-intentioned people who usually manage to do an equal amount of harm.

TO DO NOTHING IS TO DESERT HUMANKIND
AND TO PLEDGE TACIT ALLEGIANCE TO
"HUMANUNKIND."

# DIFFICULTIES AND DISASTERS

Every generation of humankind has had to suffer through its own unique difficulties and disasters. For most of humankind's existence on this planet, life has been very short and very brutish, an extended "survival camping" experience in a cave, hut, or animal-skin tent *sans* Coleman stoves, *sans* mosquito netting, *sans* canned food, *sans* all the civilized amenities that we take so much for granted when we're out "roughing it" in the wilderness. Anyone who lived beyond the age of forty was considered lucky, wise, and ancient. There were no doctors or dentists, no supermarkets, and no places to go out to for dinner. If you wanted food, you hunted for it or gathered it. If you wanted to go anywhere, you usually walked—or ran if something started pursuing you. If you wanted entertainment, you told a story or listened to one, or you sang, or you danced. And every night when you went to sleep, you could not be sure that some member of your family might not be dragged off and torn to bits by a neighborhood saber-toothed tiger in search of easy prey. This "lifestyle" went on for thousands and thousands of years. In relation to the time our species has been here, it holds the record as the dominant lifestyle of humankind. The best thing that can be said about it is that it taught people to work and live together in cooperative groups. Those who separated themselves from the group rarely survived.

As humankind became more "civilized," life for the majority continued to be short and brutish, a life of bare subsistence, miserable living conditions, and "womb-to-tomb" subjection and slavery.

And as if this were not bad enough, war after war created further hardship and suffering. Nations fought nations; empires fought empires. Alexander the Great swept through Egypt, the Middle East, and even reached as far as India. The Romans conquered most of Northern Africa, Europe, and a large part of the Middle East. These empire-building expeditions and many others like them all caused endless upheaval and loss of human life. Entire populations were made slaves by their conquerors. Entire centers of civilization were reduced to rubble.

As we "progressed," conflicting religious beliefs and rivalries, religious persecutions and crusades devoted to conversion by torture and the sword, political power struggles, and wars that would go on for decades and decades claimed endless numbers of victims—and in their path came catastrophic pestilence and famine to claim more. The Vikings, the Visigoths, the Vandals, Attila the Hun and his marauders, and Genghis Kahn and his blood-thirsty barbarians all stampeded through humankind's attempts to live in security and safety in what we now know as Europe, killing, raping, mutilating, and pillaging with gusto. And throughout the rest of much of the world the same horrible events with a different cast of conquerors and vanquished were repeated time and time again.

In addition to all these human-produced miseries and all the many epidemics of disease and times of starvation, there were geophysical disasters such as earthquakes, volcanoes, hurricanes, and floods—the most famous being the deluge which almost wiped out the entire human race.

Furthermore, up until the beginning of this century infant and child mortality rates were extremely high. Offspring who made it to the age of eighteen were considered relatively immune to any future health problems except those caused by accident, war, or epidemic, for they had already managed to survive all the "traditional" childhood diseases for which no adequate cures had been found. Modern sanitation as we know it didn't exist. Also, the work week for most people was a ten-hour, six-day-a-week drudgery with no benefits or retirement pensions.

In our own time some of our many difficulties and disasters are: the potentially destructive explosion in population; the shortsighted profit motive that places personal greed before human dignity, species' survival, and environmental quality; the invention of means for the annihilation of all life, human and otherwise; widespread world hunger; the menace of AIDS; universal ignorance and fanaticism; and the ever-increasing disparity between the "haves" and the "have-nots." And whereas our ancestors were lucky enough not to realize the full extent of the difficulties and disasters of their world, we are informed of them instantly—perhaps much to the detriment of our mental health.

Ours may seem worse to us than a saber-toothed tiger carrying off a loved one, the Romans enslaving all the men, women, and children of our entire nation, the Vikings "dropping in" to kill all the inhabitants of our little seaside village, Sherman's army burning down the old homestead and all our crops, yellow fever wasting and destroying our children or parents, or the Nazis putting most of our family in a gas chamber, but are they?

*Difficulties and disasters, **most of which we cause for ourselves individually and as members of society**, have always been the lot of every generation.*

Also, it would not be difficult to argue that the *disadvantages* of any time period were, are, or will be compensated for by the *advantages.* Look at the Indians of North America as they were before the arrival of the Europeans. True, theirs was a Neolithic culture with all it drawbacks, *but* they lived and roamed over vast tracts of undisturbed natural beauty, much of which is now "gone with the wind" and can only be seen in the paintings of Bierstadt, the Hudson River school of artists, and other early American landscape painters. They lived in harmony with their environment and did not have to see "Mother Earth" fenced off, "highwayed," railroaded, and "parking-lotted" over. They did not have to witness the ugliness of urban blight and suburban sprawl. They did not have to be subjected to watching the deterioration of air, land, and sky by the encroachment of industry. They never had to see a billboard or hear a commercial, nor have their peace disturbed by the sound of motors on a pristine lake or in the midst of a silent, snow-filled forest.

And no matter during which time period people have *lived,* they have also *died.* Death being an inevitable part of life, it's important to remember that the world ends for each one of us with our demise from this individual existence no matter how few or how many others perish with us, and no matter whether this happens due to the difficulties and disasters of the time period or in a more peaceful way.

Furthermore, in the United States, where most people enjoy a standard of living far beyond that enjoyed by Charlemagne himself, and one that would appear unbelievably carefree and utopian to a large number of our ancestors, most of us live long lives and only deal with many of these difficulties and disasters at a distance, on an intellectual and emotional rather than on a personal level.

As Charles Dickens remarked at the beginning of his novel about the French Revolution, *A Tale of Two Cities,* "It was the best of times, it was the worst of times…"

*It always has been,* and you can choose to look at the proverbial bottle with half of its contents gone and half of its contents remaining as "half-full" or "half-empty." You can look at the best aspects of our times or at the worst aspects of our times, but probably should look at both in order to keep a balanced perspective.

More to the point, you can decide to contribute to either side of the equation by helping our times be "the best" or helping our times be "the worst." And you can be thankful for all those who lived before you who made the right decision.

# THOUGHTS ON THINKING

The first thought that comes to mind when one thinks about the activity known as "thinking" is that there are too many of us who prefer to avoid it. I am not referring to what is usually labeled as "practical" thinking, such as the thinking involved in deciding what clothes to wear or which car to purchase, but I am referring to what is usually labeled as "serious" thinking, thinking that involves us in the difficult questions of life—issues such as the prevalence of evil in our world or the deeper causes of conflict among individuals, families, or societies—thinking as it is symbolized by Rodin's statue, *The Thinker*. In comparison to this kind of thought process, "practical" thinking is mere "tinkering" and could be represented by a *papier-mache* statue of a befuddled Dagwood, of "Blondie and Dagwood" comic-strip fame, fashioned as a parody of Rodin's intensely pensive philosopher.

Why do so many of us wish to avoid serious thought (which I will simply refer to as "thinking" from this point on)? I believe there are a number of very good reasons, or, more accurately, *excuses*. To begin with, thinking "hurts"; it takes sustained effort; it wrenches us out of our familiar and secure "thought" patterns and demands of us the keen observation, willingness *not* to deceive ourselves, and dogged persistence required of adventurers exploring *terra incognita.* And, as in the case of all explorers throughout history, there is no guarantee that the effort will yield any results, and every possibility that it will be dangerous. Indeed, there is every possibility that it may lead us into areas of confusion, into confronting multiple choices that all seem valid, to seeing the strength of positions that contradict our most cherished ideas. We may find that old perceptions become gray rather than black and white, that Salvador-Dali-dreamscape vistas of unresolvable, elusive, and knotty intellectual problems promising no immediate or easy resolution abound. Needless to say, we will not only find all of this bewildering and disconcerting, but we will also run the risk of reaching conclusions that those around us are not willing to accept.

*For most of us it is more convenient and less work to see things as they aren't rather than as they are,* to latch on to ready-made thought systems rather than question them, to go along with what the majority of those around us think is right—whether it be burning witches in bonfires or bombing innocent men, women, and children with napalm—in order *not* to be nonconformists or in order to free ourselves from bothering ourselves with unpopular opinions that might lead to our own ostracism. Sad but true, most of us are unwilling to even contemplate making an effort to question any part of the *status quo* that might have the slightest adverse effect on our personal security, comfort, pleasure, beliefs, income, or social standing. Should we make the effort demanded, what we discover might "rock the boat" and send us overboard without our life-jackets and without those still in the boat being willing to try to rescue us. If we examine ideas too closely, we might be torturing our minds only to endanger ourselves. And, in addition, we'll probably depress ourselves.

Do we really want to think about serious subjects, when such thinking might disturb our rose-tinted, parochial way of perceiving life? Worse yet, do we really need the mental anguish of disorienting investigations that might lead us to the embarrassing possibility of admitting that what we have always believed and lived by as being "the right way to think and act" has turned out, upon careful, honest, and painful consideration, to have been "the wrong way to think and act?" Do we really have to traumatize ourselves by intellectually struggling with the evidence offered only in order to eventually and begrudgingly surrender the Linus-blanket security of a narrow and naive view for the sober and possibly unpleasant responsibility of a more comprehensive and mature one?

The answer to all these questions, for those of us who are appalled by the overwhelming amount of *ignorance* that still dominates most human thought and behavior, is an emphatic "YES!"

*Ignorance may be blissful for the individual, but it has been, is, and will probably continue to be a major cause of unblissful suffering for humanity in general.*

Thinking may be difficult, inconvenient, and depressing, but unless more and more inhabitants of our world begin to challenge themselves to think, the *unthinkable* may become a reality, may become a final conclusion much *more* difficult, inconvenient, and depressing to deal with for those lucky or unlucky enough to survive it.

Consider, if you will, the fate of the dinosaurs. There has been much speculation about the disappearance of the dinosaurs after some 70,000,000 years of successful adaptation to life on this planet. One more theory, then, might be allowed. I believe that their extinction was due to the fact that their brains were infinitesimally small in relation to the bulk of their gargantuan bodies. The brontosaurus, the traditional plant-eating dinosaur that most people picture as representative of the typical dinosaur, is a prime example of this, weighing in at about sixty tons and boasting a brain about the size of a walnut. Whatever climatic changes, mammalian threats, terraqueous disasters, or population explosions leading to insufficient food supplies occurred, the brontosaurus and his ilk did not have the brainpower to foresee, comprehend, or deal with them.

Our tenure on this earth has been much shorter than that of the dinosaurs, but it seems highly likely that it could soon end—and for the same reason. Humanity up to this stage in its so-called evolution has developed its muscle and mass but neglected its brain. Although we have used the "practical" aspect of thinking to greatly increase our technological mass and muscle, we have used very little of our "serious" thinking ability and have often misused even the little we have been willing to employ. Until relatively recently in our history, for every one person willing to think, there have been ninety-nine who would rather face arrows or bullets than ideas, who would rather face personal extinction than thought. We seem to be doing better, but we may find ourselves to be "too late with too little."

Look at the walnut. Inside the shell are convolutions like those of the human brain. A polished walnut with half of its shell removed, sitting on your desk, would make an excellent *"memento stupiditae."*

Look at the world. All around you are evidences of *ignorance* and of the evil and suffering it causes. Some of this ignorance is directly within your sphere of influence; *some of it is even closer at hand—it is within you.* And I do not exclude myself from this observation.

Let the motto of IBM be yours: "THINK." Do some real, some serious thinking for all of us. Have the fearlessness to think for yourself and to help others think about having the same courage. "The life you save may be your own."

When the interstellar anthropologists of future ages find how large our brains were, they'll be puzzled that creatures with such large brains became extinct. What they probably won't be able to determine at first, with the evidence available to them, is that we utilized only a small percentage of our grey matter, and rarely devoted much of that small percentage to *really thinking* about important concerns and issues.

They will then move on to other speculations, such as climatic changes, bacterial threats, terraqueous disasters, population explosions leading to insufficient food supplies, and so forth, and so on.

*A New Yorker* cartoon from the Great Depression of the 1930's depicted a well-dressed, elderly businessman smoking an expensive Havana cigar in the back seat of his Rolls-Royce limousine. He can't bear to think about his problems, which include the loss of his assets in the stock-market crash of October 1929, imminent bankruptcy, and an inevitable change in lifestyle, and so he solves his "difficulties and disasters" by simply telling his impeccably dressed chauffeur: "Over the cliff, James." You see, there is a *blissful* alternative to thinking (and maybe most of us would rather "cliff it" than think)—it's called

e x t i n c t i o n.

# SECTION IV: POSSIBLE ANSWERS

*Clay Boland Jr.*

# THE ESSENTIAL STEP

*"The start of a thousand-mile journey is one step."*
—*Chinese proverb*

I've said it before, but I'll say it again.

For it is worth saying again.

And again.

Volunteers are needed.

Lots of them. Battalions of them.

If you are concerned enough, make the essential step.

If you are courageous enough, make the essential step.

If you are getting no satisfaction from the way you are living your life, make the essential step.

Step forward.

Be counted.

*The essential step is to make a commitment to make an individual contribution to the creation of a better* (rather than a worse) *world through the way you live your life. The essential step is to make a commitment to being a positive and active energy source* (rather than a neutral or negative one)—*spiritually, intellectually, morally, emotionally, socially, politically, and in every other way possible—in the world of human events and affairs.*

The world of human events and affairs, which may be an illusion, a transitory abode, or the only reality we will ever know, is, as most of us perceive it, a mess. People have trouble getting along with each other and treating each other with fairness and respect. Hatred and greed seem far more common than love and sharing. Those who are deserving seem much too often to receive less than those who are undeserving. And so it goes. The thesis is an easy one to prove. Any informed person can support it with literally hundreds of examples.

\*\*\*\*

Faced with "the way things are," you have a number of possible strategies you can put into play.

You can join those who believe the world is of no importance whatever and detach yourself from it entirely.

Or you can find yourself "attached" to it to one degree or another.

If "attached," you can find the entire experience to be more or less commonplace, tedious, unpleasant, unrewarding, or, perhaps, even unwelcome—and, of course, you will undoubtedly "infect" others with your perception.

Or you can join those who believe that the world is a miraculous phenomenon and are willing to accept both pleasure and pain in enjoying it and trying to help others appreciate it and get the most out of being in it.

You can join those who see no point in trying to ameliorate a bad situation, and who simply proceed to pursue an ultimately unsatisfactory selfishness by serving themselves at the expense of others, both through what they do and what they *fail* to do. For example, some people abandon their marriages because they are more interested in their own desires and independence than in resolving problems, which are at least partially their own, or in sharing the extremely important responsibility of raising and nurturing their own children and helping them, in as far as it is possible, to develop into well-adjusted adults. And others rarely exercise their right to vote, flatly refuse to participate in doing volunteer work in their communities, and can't even be bothered to make small donations to help support worthy endeavors, such as international charitable organizations, or even to help support the local public radio and television stations which they listen to and watch.

On the other hand, you can join those who wish to contribute something, however humble and even seemingly insignificant, to making things somewhat better; and who, therefore, purposely include in their lives an ultimately rewarding participation in creating more respect and justice for and more understanding and support of others, both through what they do and what they *don't shirk doing*. These are people who are considerate of others and their rights and needs, who make personal sacrifices in order to make difficult situations successful situations, who are willing to take on responsibilities for the well-being of others in their lives, and who realize that if concerned citizens don't make an effort to change things, others motivated more by self-concern than social or environmental concern will fill the vacuum.

You can also choose a way of looking at the world that is discouraging or encouraging.

The discouraging view is that life is "just one damn thing after another" for "no rhyme or reason."

The encouraging view is that life is one challenge after another through which we all can grow and progress to a more advanced and enlightened stage of development.

In making your choices, it is extremely important to remember that the world of human events and affairs is not the domain of some set of people "out there" called "they." The world is *all* of us, and that means *you* are as much a part of it as anyone in any group called "they." *You are a microcosm of, and an integral part of, the macrocosm called "the world."* You can choose to "look the other way," to close your eyes to this truth and consider yourself blameless while continuing to put the blame on every new "they" you can think of. Or you can accept the fact of your responsibility and make the most of your opportunity to improve things in whatever way you can, especially by improving yourself. For if you improve yourself, you improve part of "they," and therefore help improve the world for all of us.

Except for opting for detachment, the choices don't seem to be hard to make. Many people are attracted to the idea of detachment, but only a few, who some consider the wisest and holiest among us, are able to achieve it, and so almost all of use find ourselves in one way or another—"attached."

But as for the other choices, which are available to just about all of us, far too many people choose to be negative, selfish, discouraging, and "blameless." You can find adequate evidence of this on any college campus. Far too many students are apathetic about and unwilling to get involved with campus issues, activities, or government. A number of them, in addition, take only minimal and passive *interest in* or *advantage of* the classes they attend, and discourage others from showing a greater or more active interest in, or from taking a greater or more active advantage of, their educational opportunities. And when problems arise in policy affecting their "privileges" as students, or difficulties threaten their expectations of getting "good" grades in their classes, without a moment's hesitation they place the blame on administration and faculty.

I can only try to convince you that the "minority position" is the better one. I can only try to persuade you that your life will be richer if you become an active member of the "minority party," if you encourage others, if you take the responsibility to make a *positive* difference. I can only hope that you choose, or have already chosen, to be a source of encouragement, to shoulder the responsibility to *not* avoid responsibility, and to take the initiative to join those who are doing something about the *status quo* other than just criticizing it. For your own sake. For others' sake.

The options (unless you have detached yourself from the world of human events and affairs entirely) are to either step backwards, or to stand where you are, or to step forward and be counted.

The essential step is the last one mentioned, the one least made, and the one most necessary.

This is the essential, the first step available to you, to me, and to each and everyone of us in the world.

*The essential step is to make a commitment to make an individual contribution to the creation of a better* (rather than a worse) *world through the way you live your life. The essential step is to make a commitment to being a positive and active energy source* (rather than a neutral or negative one)—*spiritually, intellectually, morally, emotionally, socially, politically, and in every other way possible—in the world of human events and affairs.*

THE MORE OF US WHO TAKE IT,
THE BETTER.

# OLD-FASHIONED MORALS AND VALUES IN A MODERN, POST-INDUSTRIAL SOCIETY

In our impatience and headlong haste to be thoroughly modern, many of us have decided to dismiss much of the accumulated wisdom of all those who have lived before us, of all the countless former generations who have shaped guidelines for successful living, guidelines that were of tremendous help to those among our progenitors who understood and followed them. In this "turning our backs" on centuries of our species' past research into all aspects of human behavior and on millennia of careful and gradual development of time-proven moral standards and time-honored personal values, we may have lost sight of an excellent source of help that an increasingly greater and greater number of us need in the present and will need in the future.

We have been aided and abetted in our rebellion by some of the participants in a relatively new "research and development" endeavor, the modern science of psychology and its medical extension, psychiatry. Some of these participants, imagining that they can tidy up life by the clinical removal of old cobwebs with their new brooms, would like to wish away aspects of the human condition that cannot be wished away, realities such as remorse and guilt, and intangibles such as the human desire for more than just physical and material self-gratification.

Of course, the wiser and more mature members of this "new" profession realize that they are in actuality simply extending studies that began when the first human asked, "Who am I?" and "Why do I act the way I do?" They therefore have the intelligence and common sense to draw on, rather than discard, what others have learned before them.

After all, we have not changed appreciably in basic spiritual, mental, emotional, and psychosomatic makeup or needs from our ancestors—and we will probably not change dramatically for many a generation no matter how much we pretend to have done so; although what we make of what we are has always been evolving and shows signs of continuing to do so.

Aldous Huxley's ignoble, materialistic "utopia," that he depicts in *Brave New World,* would probably be, after the initial novelty wore off, as unsatisfying and meaningless to most of us as it was to the noble savage, John, who visits it, and who tries in vain to reconcile what he witnesses with the morals and values he has learned through living with nature, experiencing struggle and spirituality, and reading and memorizing large portions of an old, discarded, one-volume edition of the complete works of William Shakespeare that he found on the New Mexico Indian reservation where he was raised.

Nevertheless, there is more and more evidence year by year that modern humankind seems determined to keep on marching towards the "Fordian comfort and happiness" of Huxley's novel, leaving behind as excess baggage the timeless human needs that materialism and consumerism can never satisfy: the need for love; the need for transcending separateness; the need for challenge; the need for solitude and reflection; the need for self-determination, self-expression, and self-esteem; and the need for living with meaning.

And to intensify this modern predicament, we have set our recent generations loose, with very little preparation, and often with mainly just their peers to guide them, to wander aimlessly up and down the aisles of our *laissez-faire* modern supermarket of arbitrary and numerous brands of morals and values. In this "overstocked" supermarket, it is often extremely difficult to make good choices or to "get your money's worth." The large majority of products and produce sold lack nutritional value and are frequently found, after they are purchased and consumed, to be contaminated, toxic, or rotten.

And then we ingenuously wonder why so many inexperienced and unwary shoppers come home with "junk food." And then we wonder why so many get sick. What we should really wonder is how so many survive the experience.

The problem is exacerbated by the fact that a large number of the most unhealthy and poisonous items are specifically packaged to attract and allure the inexperienced, unwary buyer; whereas, the old standbys, the more nutritious products and produce that have always been around—and were staples in the days of the neighborhood grocery store, and in the days of the small-town general store, and before—are either plainly packaged or made to appear downright unattractive by those who present them to the public. And, of course, all the advertising "hype" and "glitz" is given to the former, mainly through the entertainment industry; while very little or no promotion is devoted to selling the latter.

And in some parts of the supermarket, in which the dual motivation of those in charge is "to make money and to make money" rather than "to serve customers and to make money," you can search for hours and never find anything that anybody could call "health food."

Take a trip to a video shop, and you'll see what I mean.

If you are among those who seek better "food for thought" and wish to try a new and healthier "diet," there are better places to go "shopping." Abandon the commercial "socks and violins" television programs and feature-length "give-them-circuses-if-they-won't-pay-for-bread" movies and similar sources of "mind garbage" and take the time to seek out contemporary "health food" made available by the more responsible "food merchants" still in business. Better yet, get yourself to a library—or to some thought-provoking classes or discussion groups. Study what the wisest people of the past have to say about what it means to be human.

Study the great thought systems of the past—religious and philosophical. Then turn to the new psychological ones, but keeping in mind that these last ones are "new." Study and "experience" the great artistic works of humankind—the best and most inspiring examples of architecture, sculpture, painting, music, oratory, poetry, prose, drama, dance, and cinema. In brief, investigate *all* of humankind's attempts to communicate the meaning of this experience we call life. Take whatever is useful to you in what you discover; reject whatever doesn't "ring true" for you; and question all arguments and ideas. As Descartes proposed—*to think is to exist.*

In this handbook you will find that I have drawn on many of the "moral standards" and "personal values" from the "research and development" presented and embodied in all these types of material—from the *Bhagavad-Gita* to the *New Testament;* from the *Odyssey* to *The Old Man and the Sea;* from the preludes and fugues of Johann Sebastian Bach to the ballet scores of Igor Stravinsky; from the cathedrals of the Age of Faith to the skyscrapers of New York City; from the Renaissance sculpture of Michelangelo to the Twentieth-Century paintings of Picasso: from the dramas of Euripides to the plays of Arthur Miller; from the philosophy of Plato to the psychology of Abraham Maslow; from the poetry of ancient China to the modern verse of e.e. cummings.

Although I have also included references and allusions to some contemporary works that most modern students are acquainted with, I know, from years of teaching, that they can benefit greatly from being introduced to *the "research and development" of the past which has withstood the test of time,* and of which the best "research and development" of the present is only a continuation.

I believe in and live *by* (which is different than always living *up to)* the morals and values presented and embodied in these various and varied "commentaries" on the human condition, not only because they appear time and again throughout these "commentaries," and not only because *they have been "tried out"* by millions and millions of people (basically just like you and me) *from a diversity of cultures throughout the ages and have been proven to be sound,* but also because I have learned time and again that *they "work" in my own life and in the lives of others, and that going against them doesn't.* Therefore, I see these morals and values as highly pragmatic, beneficial, and profitable for those who wish to live more full and fulfilling lives.

*They are the ways to a health that will increase your vitality, your strength, and your love of life. They can make you and all of us healthier.*

*They are the ways to a wealth that is inexhaustible, that increases by being given away, and that is available to all. They can make you and all of us richer.*

*They are the ways to the wisdom of the ages. They can make you and all of us wiser.*

*They are the ways, if you apply them in your life, of truly becoming "healthy, wealthy, and wise."*

These are the morals and values that made it possible for our ancestors for generation after generation—back through all the endlessly repeated individual dramas of being born, growing up, begetting, growing older, and soon thereafter being no longer among the quick—to make the most of life and live it with courage, dignity, and meaning.

As I have implied at the start of this essay, a number of these morals and values are not popular today, but then again, not too many people today are managing to make the most of life and live it with courage, dignity, and meaning.

It may be time for more of us to recognize that we are less "modern" than we think we are, and that *we cannot safely cut ourselves off from the best that our past has to offer.*

It may be time to take a careful look at the effects of any psychological or psychiatric theory that wantonly ignores any of the always-fundamental and never-anachronistic elements of the human psyche in an attempt to pretend we are other than we are.

It may be time to seriously assess the deleterious effects of *our popular "junk-food" culture*—a culture that *has left far too many people feeling a great emptiness* that all the amoral and valueless trash they are bombarded with cannot fill—a culture that has discouraged far too many from participation in the enthusiasm, energy, and excitement of life that is their birthright; that has rendered far too many listless, weak, "flabby," and unwilling to try to function at full or even half potential.

It may be time to look at these "old-fashioned" morals and values again. This should be easy since we all are familiar with them and are only momentarily the victims of amnesia caused by malnutrition.

To get rid of that "empty" feeling that gnaws inside you, the next time you are hungry,

TRY SOME GRANOLA!

## "REVERENCE FOR LIFE"

Dr. Albert Schweitzer, the famous humanitarian, philosopher, musician, theologian, missionary, and physician, had been struggling for months to find a solid philosophical basis for rekindling humankind's belief in ethics. He was worried that because of the weakening of religion in the Twentieth Century, and because of its replacement by faith in materialistic progress divorced from ethical values, humankind was headed toward chaos. The time was 1915, and what he saw as the first bitter results of the worship of non-ethical materialism were evident to him in the unprecedented slaughter of millions known now as World War I, the "war to end all wars."

While traveling by boat up an African river on his return to the hospital he had created in the inhospitable jungle, the answer came to him. He reports in his autobiography, *Out of My Life and Thought,* "Late on the third day, at the very moment, when, at sunset, we were making our way through a large herd of hippopotamuses, there flashed upon my mind, unforeseen and unsought, the phrase, 'Reverence for Life.'"

Each of us is conscious, says Schweitzer, that *within* us is a "will-to-live." It becomes evident to us also, he suggests, that all plants, animals, and all our fellow human beings have the same "will-to-live."

These two basic perceptions should lead us, he believes, to *an affirmation of life and a desire to promote,* in as far as we are able, *a world in which all forms of life are respected and treated with reverence.*

This affirmation, respect, and reverence lead us naturally, Schweitzer continues, to practice ethical behavior towards all other life forms.

For Schweitzer, the ethical view of life fostered by the concept of "Reverence for Life" comprehended "within itself everything that can be described as *love, devotion, and sympathy whether in suffering, joy, or effort"* (italics mine).

Schweitzer's establishment of and untiring work in his African jungle hospital are the best examples of his own affirmation of and respect and reverence for life. Indeed, his dedication to that project represents a better argument than his words ever could.

It must be pointed out, however, that there are two very important realities missing in his philosophical observation. Both have to be dealt with.

The first reality is that *if individuals do not affirm, reverence, and respect themselves, they are unlikely to affirm, reverence, and respect anyone or any other life forms.* This is a serious obstacle to Schweitzer's otherwise reasonable expectation that people should be "naturally" ethical.

The other reality missing is that *if individuals lack the imagination and intelligence to empathize; i.e., to use their minds to "see" and "feel" exactly what it must be like to be other people or other life forms, they are likely to treat both with scorn, indifference, or disrespect,* denying them just consideration and humane treatment.

Hence, it is extraordinarily important, if we wish to encourage others to be "naturally" ethical and thereby bring about and foster a more "ethical" world, that—in addition to being ethical ourselves, which is an often-overlooked *sine qua non*—we help others along the path to self-affirmation, self-reverence, and self-respect. Furthermore, we also need to help them learn the art of *empathy,* the art which I suggest elsewhere in this handbook is the key to all interpersonal relations, and which is also the key to all inter-species coexistence.

Indeed, *I believe this to be the main task* of education, not just of the relatively small amount of education that sometimes occurs in the classroom, but *of the education that every single one of us is involved in both as teacher and student every minute of every day, in the education better known as "life."*

"Reverence for Life" is very emphatically a plea for *all* life, not just for human life, and a plea for the *quality* of *all* life. Therefore, the present rapid expansion of the human species, which threatens the existence of other species and threatens the quality of all human existence (an expansion which Schweitzer could not have foreseen in 1915), is an egregious violation of this concept, even though it may seem, on first consideration, to be an application of it.

"Reverence for Life" is a beautiful and logical idea which is absolutely central to bringing under control the escalating destructive powers that threaten not only ourselves but also all other life on our planet.

The best way to implement this concept and promulgate it, as is always the case, is to encourage it in others by practicing it in your own life.

Treat others with *more* affirmation, reverence (the word is not at all too strong), and respect.

They, in turn, are more likely to feel more affirmation, reverence, and respect for themselves, and, in turn, pass that affirmation, reverence, and respect on to others and to all life forms.

Learn to empathize *more* with others.

They, in turn, are more likely to empathize with others and with all life forms.

You don't have to become a doctor in the jungles of Africa to put this idea into practice.

You can help *heal* others wherever you are and thereby help create a *healthier* world.

We all need, all life on this planet needs, a lot more

AFFIRMATION,

REVERENCE,

RESPECT,

and

EMPATHY.

# THE GOLDEN RULE

Perhaps it is "only human nature" to strain at the gnat and swallow the camel. Or, to put it more prosaically, it is easier for us to deal with details than with larger issues. This is particularly true in the case of morals and ethics; for no matter how one states it, we can deservedly be judged guilty of moral-ethical myopia. What is easy of accomplishment and less important in its implications, we "see" and argue over; what is difficult to live up to and more important in its repercussions, we are unwilling or unable to "focus on" and implement. This phenomenon reaches its most ridiculous heights in the insistence on good table manners by those among the wealthy whose lives are otherwise devoted to ruthless business practices, manipulation of political power, and the pursuit of personal corruption. Knowing which fork to use for your salad becomes more important than knowing, or caring, which tactics are ethical or unethical in a corporate takeover.

And so it is with the central axiom found in the teachings of every major world religion, *an axiom even presented as the compendium and main purpose of most of these religions.* For the very reason that it *is* central and of the greatest importance, practitioners of these religions perversely ignore it and instead trouble themselves and everybody else with minor behavioral shibboleths, dogmatic quibbles, scriptural quarrels, eschatological hypotheses, ritualistic disputes, and dietary laws. *The axiom,* of course, *is the Golden Rule.*

Since most Americans are familiar with the Judeo-Christian religious tradition, it would be appropriate to start with Judaism and Christianity, both which suggest very explicitly that *the Golden Rule is **the keystone** of religious living.* In Judaism we find the rule stated thus:

"WHAT YOU DON'T WISH FOR YOURSELF,
DO NOT WISH FOR YOUR NEIGHBOR.
*THIS IS ALL THE LAW,*
*THE REST IS ONLY COMMENTARY.*"
　　　　　　　　　　　　　—*Talmud Shabbat* (italics mine)

In Christian scripture, St. Matthew quotes Christ as having said:

"DO UNTO OTHERS ALL THAT YOU
WOULD HAVE THEM DO UNTO YOU
BECAUSE *THIS IS THE SUM*
*OF THE LAW AND THE PROPHETS.*"
　　　　　　　　　　　　　—*New Testament* (italics mine)

Obviously, not many people professing to be of either religious persuasion have paid much attention to this so supremely simple yet so extremely difficult injunction. If they had, history would contain far fewer passages of hatred, intolerance, exile, persecution, exploitation, mass-murder, and so on down the list of things no sane individuals would wish done unto them.

Many other of the world's great religions also present the Golden Rule as "the rule" that represents *the essence of religion.* In Brahman doctrine we find:

*"ALL YOUR DUTIES*
*ARE INCLUDED IN THIS:*
DO NOTHING TO OTHERS
THAT WOULD PAIN YOU
IF IT WERE DONE TO YOU."

—*Mahabharata* (italics mine)

And Muslims are warned:

*"YOU,* WHO DO NOT WISH FOR OTHERS
THE SAME AS YOU WISH
FOR YOURSELVES,
*WILL NOT BE TRUE BELIEVERS."*

—*Sunatt* (italics mine)

Again, history reveals that most followers of Brahmanism and of Islam—just as the Hebrews and the Christians—have willfully ignored, or have been unable to practice, the main teaching of their religions.

The Golden Rule appears elsewhere in the great religious teachings of the world, but without specific reference to it being the epitome of religious action. In Confucianism, we find:

"WHAT WE DON'T WANT DONE TO US,
WE SHOULD NOT DO TO OTHERS."

—*Analects*

In Taoism, it is suggested:

"HOLD AS YOUR OWN
THE GAINS OF NEIGHBORS

84

AND AS YOURS THEIR LOSSES."
— T'ai-Shang Kan-Ying P'ien

And in Buddhism, the faithful are advised:

"DO NOT OFFEND OTHERS
AS YOU WOULD
NOT WISH TO BE OFFENDED."
—*Udanavarga*

The pervasiveness of *this rule,* which *asks us to actively empathize with others and treat them as we ourselves would be treated,* is little known—which is fitting, for the rule itself is little practiced.

And yet *we all have been called* by the world's great religions *to practice active empathy;* that is, to not only empathize with others, but also to practice the charity that is the logical action which should result from that empathy. I already knew that very few of us could care less to do so, but I was amazed to discover, through research, how many of us had been asked.

The idea that *this rule is a compendium of all other important religious teachings* holds up under investigation; for if you consider the main commandments of any religion, you will readily see that, indeed, *the Golden Rule includes, in one commandment, all the others.* Hating another; cursing another; cheating another; refusing to help another in distress; denying another's legitimate freedoms and rights; dishonoring another; stealing another's goods, property, or spouse; killing another; and all the other inhumanities anyone can think of, and all the commandments against them, are included in this one rule.

Some have called the Golden Rule irrational, by which they mean we are too selfish to obey it.

Others have called the Golden Rule impossible, by which they mean we lack the strength to enact it.

But what do selfishness and weakness add up to? I would suggest that they could be summed up in the "Leaden Rule:"

"DO FOR YOURSELF,
AND, IF CONVENIENT OR PROFITABLE,
DO FOR SOMEONE ELSE
(WHO, IDEALLY, MUST FIRST BE
DESERVING OF BEING DONE UNTO)."

However, rather than deal with either extreme, it might be more sensible, and certainly more mutually supportive, to rise above the "Leaden Rule," lift our heads out of the sand-grain world of details, and at least practice the "Silver Rule." Instead of being moral-ethical nitpickers,

"LET US MAKE *MORE* OF AN EFFORT
TO DO UNTO OTHERS
AS WE WOULD HAVE THEM DO UNTO US,
EVEN IF
THEY DON'T MAKE AN EFFORT IN RETURN
(WHICH THEY PROBABLY
USUALLY WON'T,
BUT MAYBE SOMETIMES WILL)."

Or, to return to table manners: "Don't worry about which fork to use for your salad; be more concerned about not thrusting your knife into a dinner guest across the table." If you happen *not* to belong to one of the religious groups mentioned above, or to any religious group at all, you still might find the advice of the Golden Rule (or its modified form, the "Silver Rule") to be good advice. After all, you stand a fair chance of getting pretty much what you give in this life (hence the saying, "everything that goes around, comes around")—especially when what you give is negative. Moreover, the result of too many people taking refuge in minor details while living by the "Leaden Rule" has been millions and millions of cases of "lead poisoning," a large number of them fatal.

# ON THE UNDERSTANDING OF WISDOM

Wisdom comes to us from many sources. It comes to us from our culture, from our religion, from our education, from our family, from our friends, from our experiences and those of others, from our reading, from our entertainment, from our conversations, and from our observations and thoughts. Most of this wisdom is not, and has never been, profound. It is simple. Almost anyone can easily understand it— intellectually. But *living by wisdom's guidelines is another matter.* And therein lies the problem.

Most people might agree that life is short, and that they should seize the day and make the most of it. Yet most live as though life is long, and they neglect the day, acting as if they had an unending supply of days at their disposal, making very little of any of them. Most people understand that anything worthwhile gaining involves making an effort to gain it. Yet they are unwilling to subject themselves to the arduous, ongoing discipline and the constant "lifting-yourself-up-by-your-bootstraps" effort needed to overcome a myriad of obstacles and challenges in order to achieve their goals. And then, even though they know that they should learn *from* the past but not live *in* it, they spend the rest of their lives complaining about having had "bad luck," and thereby miss out on the "good luck" that is still available during the days that remain to them.

This being the case, to share wisdom with anyone is to hear the reaction: "Oh, I know that!," or "Everybody knows that!," or "That advice is older than the hills!". "That's obvious!" is what they are saying, but it's also obvious that *the very wisdom that is being offered is something that they only understand intellectually—but do not apply behaviorally.* That is why rabbis, priests, and ministers spend Sabbath after Sabbath in the Occidental world proclaiming the same "obvious" truths *over and over and over.* That is why so many dramas and novels and films and poems "teach" us the same lessons *over and over and over.* Apparently, when the subject is wisdom, we seem absolutely determined to be slow learners. We're not going to rush into anything that might involve changing our ways, especially for the better. It all sounds very fine, but *doing or living it is another matter.* ***Entirely!***

Why, even the poorly-educated Sheperdsons and Grangerfords, in Mark Twain's American classic, *Huckleberry Finn,* all admired and felt mighty nice about the uplifting and inspirational wisdom in the sermon on brotherly love given the Sunday before they managed to kill most members of each other's families during one of their more serious weekly feuds. And that was only a foreshadowing of our own national fratricide, our "Civil" War.

And so we see, time and time again, that people understand wisdom intellectually, and often admire it as theory, but most regrettably, time and time again, ignore it in practice. Yet, *the only true understanding of wisdom is to be found in its daily use.* As every carpenter knows, good tools are essential for doing good work, but if they are only admired and never touched, they are useless.

Henry David Thoreau suggested in *Walden,* one of the great early Nineteenth-Century contributions to wisdom writing, that *the only true philosophers are those who live their philosophies.* Makes sense, doesn't it? Intellectually, yes. But to do it? To really live by wisdom even if nobody else does so? Even if others criticize you for it? Even if it's inconvenient? Even if it's difficult? To live wisely and not worry about the "even if's?"

This is not so easy. But *without living your wisdom you cannot be said to truly understand it, but only to talk about it—to preach but not to practice; to profess but not to exemplify; to teach but not to learn.*

Thoreau, however, lived his life by the principle of following the dictates of wisdom. Believing that it would be unwise to allow his life to be vitiated by the accumulation of possessions that he saw all too clearly would possess him, and feeling that it would be wise to have the time to examine life carefully in order to live it intelligently, he lived his life by an economy that allowed him the freedom to live unencumbered by the unhappy pursuit of the trivia and trash of a commercial, materialistic, and frantic "civilization," that allowed him the time to examine the nature around him and the nature within him.

He disagreed with our declaring war against Mexico, feeling that the war was unabashed, expansionist aggression that would bring more slave states into the Union. He expressed this disagreement by going to jail rather than paying his taxes to support what he called an "immoral" war. Since wisdom told him that *to support that which you don't believe in is wrong,* he did more than talk about his disagreement. He acted. When his friend, Ralph Waldo Emerson, asked him what he was doing in jail, Thoreau asked Emerson what *he* was doing *outside*—since they both shared the same sentiments.

Throughout his life Thoreau *lived* his wisdom: despite the disappointment of Emerson, who felt that Thoreau could have had a brilliant, more "acceptable" career but instead chose to be "captain of a huckleberry party"; despite the criticism of his neighbors, who considered him a loafer and hardly better than a bum (even though he did work part-time as a surveyor and handyman, and helped out now and then with the family pencil business); and despite his lack of so-called "worldly" success as a writer and would-be lecturer during his lifetime.

The result, however, for Thoreau himself, was anything but disappointing. He could look back at a fulfilling life—a life that he had *lived.* Even though his life was relatively short, it was nonetheless more rewarding than many other longer lives, for *he had lived by the wisdom he had learned.* When he was on his deathbed, a friend asked him whether he made his peace with God. Henry answered, "I didn't know we had quarreled."

True. They probably hadn't. But most of us do. The "quarrel," to read it in terms of wisdom both religious and secular, is between what we *say* we understand and what we actually *do*—between our intellectual comprehension and our behavior which loudly contradicts it.

Part of the examined life—the only life, as Socrates and other wisdom seekers and teachers have suggested, worth living—is a daily examination of how you have done in *applying* the wisdom you have learned. The point of this is not to put yourself down or to puff yourself up but simply to objectively examine how the experiment called "your life" went for one more day, to examine how you are *doing* in relation to what you are *saying.* Being sure to consider both negative and positive events (and not just the former), you can look at the results, draw your conclusions, and benefit from your findings. Be warned, however:

> *THERE IS A LONG, DIFFICULT WAY*
> *BETWEEN "SAY" AND "DO,"*
> *BUT IT'S THE ONLY WAY TO TRUE*
> *WISDOM.*

Meanwhile, the next time someone offers you some timeless wisdom for your benefit, be sure you're *living* the advice before you respond: "Oh, I know that!"

> IF YOU'RE NOT LIVING IT,
> YOU DON'T *KNOW* IT.

If you truly *know* it, that knowledge will show for all to see in everything you do, and nobody will feel the need to give you the advice.

And, not too incidentally, if you live your wisdom, your living it will do more to teach it to others than all the words in the world repeated *over and over and over* ever can, for

*EXAMPLE IS THE BEST TEACHER,*
*AND WISDOM IS THE BEST THING*
*IT CAN TEACH.*

# ON BEING RIGHT; OR, "I'D RATHER BE WRONG!"

"Who is right?"

Too many friends, couples, families, and neighbors find themselves emotionally entangled in this contentious, age-old question on a regular and almost predictable basis.

Look, for example, at the conflicts in a marriage. In these conflicts, both parties fight over being right like two starving dogs snarling over a choice steak bone. Or one party will silently suffer from what are perceived as the other party's wrong attitude and behavior, waiting like a wounded lion in ambush for the hunter who has shot at it, waiting for the opportune moment to savagely counterattack and be revenged.

This kind of situation *cannot* usually be remedied by changing friends, lovers, partners, becoming part of a new family, or moving to a new neighborhood. *As long as everyone insists on being right about practically everything,* every couple will be an "odd couple," and every possible combination or permutation of family and neighbors "odd bedfellows," because *everyone will be at odds with everyone else most of the time.*

For instance, escalating the "conflict" to the neighborhood level, I could offer my own, small, rural subdivision, whose residents have recreated an excruciatingly perfect parody of the animosities and mutual aggressions of Europe in the first half of this century, although the resultant bloodshed and destruction are more figurative than literal, and the sporadic outbreaks of open hostilities more comedic than tragic. I have found very little evidence to convince me that other neighborhoods are much different, whether at the local or international level.

Homeowners' meetings, in particular, demonstrate the problem. These meetings are always extremely entertaining and lively, but rarely productive, because now the couples who have been contending at home can join a larger "free-for-all" in which every individual is right and all the others partially or totally "off-the-mark."

And so it goes—at every level of human interaction.

And although this kind of controversy does more to deprive us than it does to help us thrive, *we are obsessed by it.* Some of the more belligerent among us have even come to consider conversation and controversy as one and the same transaction. This is particularly evident in the case of conversations about *politics, religion,* and *sex.*

For generations, people have been warned of the dangers of discussing these highly controversial issues.

Why?

They have been warned because all participants in such discussions have made "serious," personal "investments" in their beliefs on these complex subjects and have convinced themselves that, whereas everyone else is benighted, they are enlightened. And when all participants in a discussion are convinced they are right, none can tolerate the awkwardness of this "impossibility." After all, how can more than one position be "right?" Benjamin Franklin found a perfect image for this phenomenon, likening all of us to people wandering through a dense fog, each wanderer thinking, "Where I am, one can see clearly, but all the others, poor souls, are terribly lost in the mist that envelops them and clouds their vision."

Therefore, all the participants, believing they alone are enlightened, or that only they see things clearly, fight to avoid the embarrassment of being proven wrong about even the smallest detail. They fight to avoid making the unthinkable admission that *what they perceive as right is something they have never thought through thoroughly and/or have never been able to fully comprehend,* BUT SIMPLY—out of laziness, conformity, convenience; as a result of physical constitution, physiological influences, psychological makeup; due to social position, economic standing, racial background, generation membership; and/or because of nationality, indoctrination, parental pressure, lack of adequate information, and so on down the list—HAVE ACCEPTED.

*They fight to avoid the embarrassment of appearing to be fools!!!*

But there is a holiday from all of this. Once a year, on April 1st, we're all allowed to demonstrate what fools we all are by getting others to believe that which isn't so. And then we laugh at them. And unless they are hopeless, they laugh too. And, of course, they have the liberty to return the favor. But that's just once a year. Just as once a year, on December 25th, we allow ourselves to give to others; once a year we allow ourselves to realize the foolishness of believing we are right—about anything and everything.

Both days should be multiplied by three-hundred-and-sixty-five every year. For some people they are. But, at present, for most of us they are just quaint, odd customs that are irritating nuisances disturbing our typical "bah-humbug" and "it's-my-opinion-and-it's-very-correct" routine.

*Like so many children quarreling over whose parents are best, we shout and hit out at each other with tears of wanting-to-believe-what-we-say-is-true in our eyes.*

*I'd rather grow up.*

*I'd rather achieve the maturity to admit that I could be wrong about anything or everything than add to the wrongs that we already have created by our insistence on being right.* It is only natural and very important to consider issues of right and wrong, but I do not wish to insist that I have, or anyone else has, the definitive answer to anything. *Hubris* is just another name for ignorance. And using "might" to "prove" you are "right" is the last resort of the playground bully.

*I'd rather be wrong* than join any group that claims to have found the one and only right "way" in politics, religion, or even sex. It's not impossible to consider that there are many "ways"—some right for some and some right for others. And yet most of us are not willing to accept this idea. For most of us this is blatant and dangerous "heresy." But if this is "heresy," what name are we to give to the blatant and dangerous position it challenges? For the terrible, barbaric, anti-humankind result of our nonacceptance has been—mainly in politics and religion, but also to some degree in the area of sexual mores—desperate, costly, and destructive power struggles that have caused some or all of the following, ourselves-created "plagues": bitter hatred, divisive intolerance, mindless fanaticism, ruthless persecution, wholesale maiming and murder, generation after generation of war, genocide, and finally, looming ahead of us in the very near future, the awful, truly unthinkable possibility of destroying everybody and everything to prove:

*WE ARE RIGHT!!!!!!!!!!!!!!!!!!!!!!!!!!!!!!!!*

And the expulsion from Eden will be completed.
Forever.

And the Babel of disagreement silenced.
Forever.

And Armageddon fought and finished.
Forever.

One can only hope that we are witnessing the Aesopian race of the tortoise and the hare, the hare being the very advanced and highly sophisticated technology of mass destruction and mutual slaughter, and the tortoise being human education; for we have a lot to learn and not much time to learn it. Right now, we, in our development of the *humility, empathy, and maturity* we are sorely lacking, seem to be far behind in the race, dragging ourselves along slowly and reluctantly, encumbered by our past mistakes rather than having learned from them, and not having made much progress in moving forward from the Neolithic cave that was our starting point; while the hare flies along, guided by computer and radar, towards the finish line, showing no signs of wanting to take a nap, and oblivious to the implications of an easy and very probable victory.

We need to get going. We need to catch up. We need to get ahead as humans in our race with the Frankenstein technology of annihilation that we in our madness have created.

*Rather than creating enmities and enemies and possible "geocide" over politics, religion, and even sex—and other controversial subjects—it might be more beneficial to and intelligent for everyone to be glad for any political, religious, sexual, economic, philosophical, educational, social, or parental system which inspires people to be more loving, empathetic, compassionate, informed, tolerant, decent, dignified, self-fulfilled, and self-respecting than the majority of* us are at present—no matter how bizarre such a system may seem to be.

****

The elephant is an elephant even though the blind "wise" men in the ancient story who were placed here and there on its body described it in different ways depending on what they found—whether it was its trunk, its leg, its ear, or some other part of its enormous anatomy. So it is with being right on any subject. We might be right to some extent but unable to "see" enough to claim to be totally right. No doubt the blind "wise" men later dismembered each other in a heated argument about whether the elephant was a trunk, a leg, an ear, or whatever. But that predictable folly was left out of the story as not being suitable for children to hear.

Look back at the infamous beliefs people have held to be "irrefutable"—such as believing that certain racial groups were meant to be slaves while other racial groups were meant to be their masters, or that rulers were semidivine and therefore should be worshipped and obeyed without question, or that human sacrifice was necessary for propitiating the gods. These "irrefutable" beliefs of the not-so-distant past should teach all of us some much-needed humility about believing we are right—about anything and everything.

It seems to me that the great irony of thinking we are *absolutely right* is that, in most cases, it has led us to attitudes and behaviors that have been *absolutely wrong*.

The odds are that most people will believe I am absolutely wrong in thinking they are not absolutely right. But it may be right to hope that I'm wrong. In the name of humanity, and in reverence for our unique, terraqueous planet and all the other life forms on it,

### *I'D RATHER BE WRONG!!!!!!!!!!*

# ONE IN FIVE BILLION<sup>*</sup>

> *"If one by one we light*
> *our individual lights, we can*
> *illuminate the whole world."*
> —*Koichi Tohei*

As one of the five billion human inhabitants of the modern world, your chances of being powerful, wealthy, or famous are statistically minute. If you live in a modern industrialized country, your power may seem to be limited to your vote, your wealth to your ability to feed, clothe, and shelter yourself and/or your family, and your fame to the annual listing of your name in the local telephone directory. Or you may be less fortunate.

But no matter what your situation is, YOU COUNT.
Whether you think so or not, YOU COUNT.
Whether you want to or not, YOU COUNT.

*Every single person,* indeed, *either adds to or subtracts from the power, wealth, and fame of the species.* Every single person helps humankind succeed or hurries it on to possible failure. And, since humankind has assumed the stewardship of our planet, everyone of us adds to or subtracts from the quality and survival of our entire biosphere and all its billions

---

<sup>*</sup> Approximate world population, 1990.

and billions of other co-inhabitants, and all of its air, water, and land. *We are all accountable—every single one of us.*

Yes, YOU COUNT.
YOU cannot help but COUNT.
Not **whether** you do but **how** YOU will COUNT is the question.

The question is, *"Does or will your life represent, when all the pluses and minuses are tallied, a positive or negative total on the larger balance sheet?"*

Obviously, the worst case imaginable would be a world of five billion individuals producing *negative* results, creating a deficit beyond repayment; each, through ignorance of personal responsibility, plunging the world into spiritual, political, moral, emotional, physical, and ecological bankruptcy.

And obviously, the best case possible would be a world of five billion individuals producing *positive* results, creating a profit from which all can benefit; each, through recognition of personal responsibility, bringing about a world of spiritual, political, moral, emotional, physical, and ecological solvency or even surplus.

It certainly is easier to consider that we are moving more toward the worst case than toward the best. It is also possible to consider that this has always been so. But now that the world's population is expanding to a dangerous level of overcrowding, causing overuse of our limited resources and a deterioration in the quality of life for many; and now that our technology, while creating numerous blessings for humanity, has unwittingly aided this growth and also, in the name of military preparedness, created threats that could end all existence on this planet; the continuation of a balance sheet constantly more in the red than in the black should give everyone pause to look more carefully at *individual accountability.*

*All of us need to be aware that every single one of us counts.* Nevertheless, most of us like to look at the statistics, at "the odds against us," if you will, and say that we can't possibly make a difference, and therefore we don't try. And as a result, since, no matter what we think, we can't help but make a difference, we make the *wrong* difference.

Both those who don't vote despite having the privilege to do so and those who vote poorly informed offer excellent examples of this kind of thinking and its ultimate results—a government of the politicians, by the politicians, and for the politicians.

The litter along our highways and beaches offers a more visible instance of making the *wrong* difference. People who litter must think, if they are thinking at all, that their small "contribution," thrown out of a car window or tossed out of a boat, can have very little impact on the landscape or beachscape. But how quickly all these individual "contributions" add up, creating an aesthetic and ecological nuisance, a visual and unnatural clutter.

In a world in which hunger still prevails, where oppression is the rule rather than the exception, and ignorance is the lot of the majority of humankind; it becomes even more pressing for those with enough food to eat, with the blessings of freedom, and with sufficient education to realize the impact each of us has on our world, to act.

**** 

In the long run, both the fortunate and the unfortunate can do something to help lessen the problems of world malnutrition, exploitation by oppression, and lack of universal education. Neither group by itself can complete the job. The venture must eventually be a cooperative one.

But first things first. *All these problems will remain as they are unless the basic attitudes of the "victims" and the "victimizers" and of those who think that they have nothing to do with the problems change.* Until we all realize that *we are all involved in all problems,* until we all realize that *our attitudes and priorities and goals are often the causes of effects we blame others for,* the problems will continue, and we will all continue to feel that there is nothing that we can do about anything.

We will all just shrug our shoulders and say, "That's the way it is," and then turn around and immediately do or say something that helps it continue to be that way.

*Such unawareness and our refusal to accept our responsibility in influencing "what is" eventually come back to us and/or those close to us in the form of most unwelcome consequences:* a favorite lake declared devoid of life; a neighbor stabbed or shot; a mother, wife, sister, or daughter raped; a father, husband, brother, or son wounded or killed in war. Our refusal also lives with us in the form of a "conscience" that can be quieted but never totally silenced.

*Look at your own attitudes, priorities, and goals.* It should not be too difficult to trace the effects of these on the world you see around you. It may be proper and fitting to "point the finger" at the participants in the most recent financial swindle of public or corporate funds, but you should also look at your own willingness to "fudge" or even cheat in money matters such as your income tax. It may be good "social consciousness" raising to criticize the rich landowners in Latin America for hiring armed thugs to keep the poor frightened, submissive, and underpaid, but you should not neglect, in so doing, to look at your own selfishness and consider how you also take advantage of others. It may be necessary to periodically remind each new generation of the horrible inhumanities practiced at Auchswitz during World War II, but, at the same time, you should not overlook your own additions to the problems of prejudice through "harmless" jokes, biased remarks, and not speaking up when you should. In all cases, the extreme example may be worse in its consequences, but it is cut from the same cloth as the seemingly minor one—which is simply an earlier and prerequisite stage of its more flagrant manifestation. One may be worse than the other, but *both stem from the same attitudes, priorities, and goals.*

The best way to deal with the columns of red ink on the balance sheets of humanity, then, is *not* to detach yourself and pretend that you are an uninvolved spectator but to accept your own complicity and to personally add to the columns of black ink. *Bringing to* the world around you more love and less hate, more concern and less indifference, more helping and less shirking, more sharing and less selfishness, more understanding and less stereotyping, more respect and less dehumanization, more awareness and less ignorance; more, in brief, of what is needed and less of what is polluting our attitudes, our lives, and our world—these are the essential personal actions needed before any true and lasting improvements can be made.* This is what it means, as I have suggested before, to *"live the world you want."*

When you start to live it, watch the "emptiness" in your life and in the lives of others start to disappear. To live as an "isolato" is to be gnawed to death by the cancer of "self with a small 's.'" To acknowledge that "we're all in this together" and must help each other is to find *meaning* and *purpose* in your life.

Volunteer to do some work with children, or in a school, or for the elderly, and reconnect yourself with the human race. In so doing you will regain your "health" and your self-respect, and will help maintain a balance of "good" power in the world.

But, more crucially, internalize the attitudes that would be involved in such activities and "live" them everyday in everything you do. For since *the character of the human affairs of our world is essentially a reflection of the character of each one of us,* as each one of us "goes," so "goes" the world. The news media, however, seem mainly to be interested in our negative traits and their effects—since these make "better" copy. But our positive traits and their effects are "active" all of the time also, even if usually in a less sensational way. If they weren't, things would be a whole lot worse than they are.

Rather than being depressed and incapacitated by the cruelties, inequities, and stupidities evident everywhere one looks, do something positive. To be depressed and incapacitated is to surrender to that which can, if you allow it to do so, overwhelm you. *Weltschmerz* will always be with us, but it should goad us on to action rather than cripple us with melancholy.

Consider the wisdom of the old saying, "It's better to light one candle than to curse the darkness," and recall the heartening experiment performed years ago in a darkened football stadium when *each* of the fifty thousand participants lit a candle and transformed dark night into brilliant day. What more evidence does one need of the power of individuals to change the world? Imagine five billion candles lit all at once in a benighted world!

Light your candle now.

Let it shine—not under a bushel, but for all to see and for all to see by.

Others will start to join you, and we'll all see and feel better than we do now.

No one can deny that you are only one person out of five billion, but that's also true for all the other four billion, nine-hundred and ninety-nine million, nine-hundred and ninety-nine thousand, nine-hundred and ninety-nine human beings living here with you. Does this really impress you as an argument for nobody doing anything?

All reform, as Thoreau astutely pointed out, begins with self-reform.

*All reform starts with you*

And the best time to start is right now.

The world's accounting ledgers are always opened.

WHY NOT "MAKE YOUR LIFE
ADD UP TO SOMETHING"
AND HELP
BALANCE THE BOOKS?

# PARADOXES

Call it the *easy* way if you wish, but it is the most difficult. It is far easier to join the Peace Corps, spend two years in a native village helping others, and then return to "normal" life feeling that you have "done your bit," than it is to be a living example of "peacefulness" and "helping" everyday of your life.

Call it the *small* way if you wish, but it is the largest. All the political remedies imposed from above are only temporary and bound to be ineffective, like bandages on a wound that festers on and on, unless more and more individuals realize they are integral parts of both the problems they face and the solutions they desire.

Call it the *apolitical* way if you wish, but it is the most political. It is an exponentially growing movement of individuals throughout the world who are tired of the hypocrisy of politicians who preach one thing and practice another, individuals who have therefore decided to *live* the policies by which they believe the world should and can be governed. These individuals can be found everywhere, and more and more people join them all the time. Through the way they live their lives they elect to be "politically" active every day of the year—not just on election days. They are the first of the new "cosmopoliticians" of the future. They are the *avant-guarde* of a truly *new* world order.

*Clay Boland Jr.*

# NOT THE BEST OF ALL POSSIBLE WORLDS BUT A BETTER ONE

Leibnitz, a highly renowned mathematician and philosopher of the Eighteenth Century, concluded that if the vast heavens of innumerable celestial bodies moving in orderly, mathematical majesty "worked"; and the minute and intricate animate splendors scampering busily about in the recently discovered cosmos of the microscope "worked"; then the world in between and the creatures in it, including ourselves, must also "work." The entire system was, as he expressed it, "the best of all possible worlds," its "gears" turning and meshing with the precision of a well-made Swiss clock—every inanimate object, every animate being, every cause, every effect, every life, and every death an integral and necessary part of its perfect functioning.

Possible? It could be. The handiwork of creation evident in the starlit night skies and on the microscope slide is ingenious and endlessly fascinating; yet, in its most mysterious aspects, beyond our limited human comprehension. The same can be said about the world in between. The same can be said about "the *way* of the world"—the human way.

And if the universe and everything in it, including ourselves, is beyond our ability to completely understand, it is not impossible to believe that everything, including ourselves, "works," and that this is, indeed, "the best of all possible worlds."

If, to give one example, you are willing to entertain the idea that this world may be a school in which we are meant to learn, to be tested, and through our experiences to grow spiritually, then there is little doubt that the world serves this purpose more than adequately. Perhaps, to follow this hypothesis a bit further, the school is as harsh as it is because we are all lackadaisical and inattentive students who prefer delinquency to discipline. Or to shift to a somewhat similar but more physical metaphor, we may not enjoy the cosmic commando course, but running it may be the only way we will ever get in shape.

Voltaire, a highly renowned author and philosopher, also living in the Eighteenth Century, attacked Leibnitz's view in his memorable, and still widely read novelette, *Candide.* Against a vividly and satirically depicted background of natural catastrophes, such as the earthquakes of the mid-1700's that decimated the population of Lisbon; and equally tragic, human-created cruelties, such as the wanton slaughter of thousands in land and sea battles and the ghastly *autos-de-fe* of the Spanish Inquisition; Voltaire presents a world populated by a rogues' gallery of vicious, villainous, treacherous, greedy, lustful, manipulative, and totally degenerate human beings. This is the world in which Candide, our naive and unsuspecting hero, must test the theory that this is "the best of all possible worlds," the philosophical *weltanschauung* taught to him by his mentor, Pangloss, a follower of Leibnitz.

Every occurrence in Voltaire's encyclopedic presentation of the world's evils is designed to undermine our protagonist's belief in his cherished philosophical assumption. Many ludicrous, awful, and absurd causes and effects later, Candide finally concludes that, although Pangloss' philosophy *might* be true in some way not quite clear to him, he would be better off if he were to "cultivate his own garden." And this he does, by taking responsibility for his own actions and his own life, and by helping others who wish to join him do the same. In so doing, he creates, even though only on a small scale, in the midst of what may be the best, or maybe the worst, or maybe a combination of the best and worst of all possible worlds, a *better* world.

The higher realms of philosophical speculation, scientific investigation, and theological apologetics await you if you wish to pursue the seemingly imponderable problem of whether our world is "the best of all possible worlds," or the worst, or both. The question is intriguing and tantalizing. It has been asked by every intelligent human being who has ever lived. It is a question worthy of serious thought and discussion. It is a question worthy of many possible theoretical answers.

However, meanwhile back in the world of daily living, you can *answer* the question, if you wish to do so, in a more meaningful way, by "cultivating your own garden" as Candide did. By improving yourself, by making yourself the best of all possible selves you have the potential to be, or at least by making yourself a better person, you can make some part of this world better for yourself and for those around you.

"Cultivate your own garden," then, is good practical advice. It "works." Most of us may never accept this world as the *best,* but each of us can endeavor to avoid making this world *worse,* for we can apply ourselves to the individual task of making it *better* by making ourselves *better.*

Involvement in community services, charitable organizations, environmental clubs, and political movements can be an important use of your time, energy, and money if these have been formed to help create a better world. Membership in destructive cults, hate-oriented organizations, anti-conservation groups, or political parties devoted to serving the few and hoodwinking the many would be, on the other hand, your personal choice to help in the creation of a worse world.

I hope your decision is to join the former and not the latter.

But before you move into the larger arena, and even when you are there, remember that *the individual is the essential unit and component of all change.* Leaders at an anti-war rally shouting with hatred at each other or even at their absent opponents have not done their *home*work. For reform, like charity, begins at home, and *we cannot bring about in the world that which we have not first brought about in ourselves.*

AS LONG AS WE NEGLECT OUR OWN GARDENS, WE WILL ONLY HELP CREATE A WORLD FULL OF UNSIGHTLY WEEDS.

And even if this world *is* "the best of all possible worlds," a possibility that shouldn't be discounted, I believe not too many people would object to anyone trying to make it a bit better.

A well-tended garden is always a pleasure to behold. Furthermore, gardening in and of itself is good for the spirit.

# EARNING AND MAINTAINING YOUR RIGHTS; OR, OF PRIDE AND PREJUDICE

Much has been said about the fact that people need to stand up for their rights, but little is ever mentioned about the fact that they must first *deserve* to stand up for them, and then must subsequently remain standing and attentive if they wish to *preserve* them. Inalienable rights are, whether we like it or not, only inalienable for those who have earned them the hard way and are willing to constantly maintain and defend them.

The story of so-called "minority" groups (some of which, like women, have actually been "majority" groups) moving from both the obvious and less obvious forms of bondage to relative freedom throughout the history of the United States of America has demonstrated time and again that this is the case. Despite all the egalitarian rhetoric in our official documents, every "minority" group has been "enslaved" in one way or another and victimized by virulent prejudice as its painful and almost unbearable initiation into "the land of the free and the home of the brave." Each has then had to show itself worthy of freedom, and each has had to continue the unending struggle of keeping that freedom.

Perhaps too few of us have looked carefully enough at those last words of our national anthem, "the land of the free and the home of the brave." That stirring phrase addresses the situation directly, for *you cannot be free unless you are also willing to be brave,* unless you have the courage to handle the responsibility of freedom and to pay the cost of keeping it. For example, adolescents growing up within the mutual interdependence of their own family need to be willing to deal with the inconvenience, effort, and probable suffering of being brave, of making their own, personal (even-though-for-practical-purposes-somewhat-limited), fledgling declarations of their independence as family members developing into responsible and mature individuals worthy of respect, capable of respecting others, and willing to contribute and share. Otherwise, they will find themselves less emancipated than they would like to be or should be. Of course, if they're developing in the opposite direction, they are only inviting the deterioration of the few rights they already have. In that case, their bravery will be more effective if devoted to the task of turning things around first, of gaining their own self-respect before asking for respect from others.

But back to the larger family, our nation. Indentured servants were among our first "minority" groups and were literally slaves, though the term was not used to describe them. In a metaphorical sense, they set the pattern for all the groups that followed them from within or without our nation, for *they* had *contracted themselves to work in order to gain their freedom.* At the end of the time specified in their contracts, these servants were free to strike out on their own if they so desired. African war prisoners were our first official "slaves," and, in addition to being "indentured" for life, rather than for seven or more years, were originally, because of their economic usefulness, denied even the means, such as literacy, education, and social mobility, to stand up for themselves and gain their freedom.

After the first two groups, the indentured servants and the African slaves, there came group after group, each treated as inferior, each initially "employed" as "wage slaves," and each subjected, as were the servants and slaves before them, to prejudice: the Germans, the Irish, the Jews, the Italians, the Polish, the Swedes, the Chinese, the Russians, the Puerto Ricans, the Mexicans, and all the other "huddled masses yearning to breathe free." Being uprooted from one's homeland was awful enough, but what awaited these people upon arrival was often worse, except for one key factor—here there was *hope,* if not for them, then for their children; if not for their children, then for their grandchildren. Yes, there was hope, but it wasn't printed on their immigration papers, and it wasn't stamped under the "foreign" names that most immigration officials couldn't spell correctly. And although it was symbolized in time by the Statue of Liberty standing more sternly than maternally in New York harbor, it was only available, as was the freedom promised, to those who struggled to take advantage of it. And that is still the case here and everywhere in the world. *Hope is hopeless without effort. Freedom is not free, and "slavery" is the price of not being willing to pay for it.*

Nonetheless, I love America. I love America because it's "impossible." According to the standards of the world, so many people of so many diverse backgrounds should not be able to live together successfully. And yet, even though we're moving at a glacial rate, we're slowly inching our reality closer and closer to our rhetoric. As Harry Truman put it, "The impossible takes a little longer," and I'm still rooting for the home team, for that good old *"e pluribus unum."* For if we can make it, maybe the world can too.

Ironically, it was often through war, the ultimate form of slavery, that these groups (and the American Indians, who were here before all of them) made progress towards gaining the freedom promised to them but rarely delivered. Many of their members "paid the full price" for an idea that they hoped would eventually apply to them just as it already applied to the more established and more fortunate sons and daughters of liberty.

And the ones that returned had not only earned their rights the hard way but were more inspired than ever to get them. (When you're willing to die for your country, you are not willing to put up with being told you are not welcome to take your family to dinner in a restaurant in your own hometown.) Equally, if not more importantly, they had earned their own self-respect.

For one of the most damning and damaging effects of prejudice in this country, or in any country, is that its victims begin to believe it. And *you can't earn anyone else's respect unless you first gain your own respect and develop the ability to respect other people no matter how mistaken you may believe their perceptions are.* As for the victimizers, I think you will find that the less self-respect they have for themselves, and the more fear they have of losing an undeserved "superiority," the more they will tend to hold on to their prejudices.

What we are talking about is *work.* To earn and maintain your rights in any situation—family, peer group, community, or nation—is work. The name of the game is, as in any worthwhile endeavor, "no pain, no gain." The name of the game is *courage,* for if your cause is right, fear isn't. The name of the game is *persistence.*

It would be nice if life were like the fairy tales that children love so much in which the enemy is always externalized and success is always guaranteed before the story ends. In real life, you are part of the enemy and success is not guaranteed before the story ends for you, and total success is not even guaranteed for your children or grandchildren. For *the enemy is* not a person or a group but *an attitude* that is poisoning both your mind and the minds of those you have labeled as your enemies. This attitude, standing between you and your rights, is *prejudice:* a "pre-judgment" that you neither deserve nor can maintain those rights. Both you and they are the slaves of this attitude, and it will take work to change it.

So, how do you go about it? The well-known "secret" is that

## YOU CAN'T CHANGE ANYONE ELSE UNLESS YOU CHANGE YOURSELF.

Or to put it another way, the only *effective* way to change anyone else is to change yourself. Therefore, if you are dealing with an attitude, start with your own. *Don't buy into an attitude by accepting it in your own*

119

*attitude towards yourself.* If others don't respect you, that's their problem. If you don't respect yourself, they'll never solve their problem. If you fulfill their low expectations of you, their low expectations will remain unaltered. You will empower and reinforce the true enemy—their attitude. On the other hand, if you fulfill your own expectations of what you can be and can do, and if you proceed to deal with others without "putting yourself down" (and without putting them down unless you wish to reverse and continue the problem rather than alleviate it), the expectations of others will change, perhaps gradually, perhaps even imperceptibly, but nevertheless in the right direction.

*If you have a chip on your shoulder, do the work necessary to remove it.* By keeping it there, you are only inviting others to "read" it as an epaulet of inferior rank. *Deal with others as if they are just other "versions" of yourself, for that is all they are despite whatever else they may think they are.*

And since prejudice is an inescapable part of life, don't think you'll ever totally eradicate it. You never will, not even in yourself. But keep wearing the attitude down, erode its power, explode its myths. Above all, forget Utopia; it's just another fairy tale. A better reality, however, is possible and worth the effort.

Some specific tactics in the "war" against prejudice are tactics that also dramatically increase self-esteem. These strategies, which have been proven to be highly effective for many of the groups mentioned earlier, are achievement, "dressing for success," and the effective usage of standard vocabulary and language. All these have "worked" because they foster self-respect and elicit the respect of others. Academic, business, professional, military, artistic, athletic, or any kind of personal achievement can help bolster your self-esteem and can help erode the power of prejudice. Dressing in the style of the successful members of your society, or in any style that makes you feel good about yourself, also makes a statement that helps your self-prestige and weakens the grip of prejudice. And learning the language of those who would treat you as a lesser person is not a "sell-out" but a "sound" investment. In so doing, you demonstrate that you too can think and express yourself effectively and intelligently, and, better yet, can do so in more than one language—yours and theirs. For many people, believing that other languages and regional variations different than their own sound inferior to the language and usage they associate with "superiority," or at least with "belonging," are convinced that others not using their standard language, usage, and vocabulary are below-standard people. This may seem to be a very faulty and unfair generalization, but it is the way most people think.

Finally, *who are the victims of prejudice? We all are.* Some of us more than others. But no one can escape. No one. You are the victim of all those who will try to put you down for anything and everything under the sun or the moon: your age, your sex, your name, your skin color, your hair, your eyes, your nose, your teeth, your weight, your height, your religion, your politics, your employment, your nationality, your "anything."

And, *who are the victimizers? We all are.* Some of us more than others. No one is exempt. No one.

Prejudice is one of the uglinesses of being human.

Don't buy into it.

Lessen it in yourself,
> in your attitude toward yourself.

Lessen it in yourself,
> in your attitude toward others.

Lessen it in others, by not reacting to or going along with their inability to see you as the responsible, contributing, and mature person that you're earning and maintaining the right to be seen as and treated as.

Have the courage to stand up for your rights, to let your voice be heard, to take action that "counts," but first make the effort to *earn* those rights, and after you get them be sure to *guard* them bravely.

And if after making the effort and getting and keeping your own self-respect, you still find that there are "holdouts" who seem to begrudge you a "fair trial," don't be discouraged. In time, they will change.

But meanwhile, you will have the very important satisfaction of *not* being subjected to suffering prejudice from the one person you will be spending the rest of your life with—*yourself.*

And that, in and of itself, is worth gaining and maintaining.

Perhaps that is the most valuable "right" you or anyone else can ever win—

> the right to be proud of yourself,
> the right to your own personal self-respect,
> the right to freedom from self-inflicted
> PREJUDICE.

## SELF-GOVERNMENT

$P$lato, disgusted with the politics and politicians of his time, created an academy to educate and train the ideal leader, the philosopher ruler. The philosopher ruler would be one who, having carefully studied wisdom, would live and judge wisely; one who, having carefully studied the art of thinking, would practice reason and forethought in decision-making; and one who, having undergone rigorous training in the demanding discipline of self-government, could, therefore, with understanding and without hypocrisy, undertake the governing of others.

Plato felt that a philosopher would be a better ruler than a politician, for he believed that a philosopher would tend to work from a basis of sound moral principles; whereas a politician would more than likely either base most decisions and actions on popular expediency or, worse yet, on personal whims and desires.

In actual practice, leaders throughout history have been motivated by all three considerations: moral, popular, and personal. The greater the leader in regard to benefiting humankind through example and action, the more the leader has been willing to sacrifice the lesser end of the scale for the higher. Mahatma Gandhi is an excellent example of a great leader motivated by higher goals, for he was willing to disregard popular expediency as well as personal whims and desires in his crusade for moral justice. His strength was such that he almost single-handedly inspired his countrymen to passively resist the domination of the British Empire and free their country from oppressive colonization.

Ironically, even infamous leaders, such as Adolph Hitler, while centering their policies on popular and personal gratification, whatever the cost to others who are the victims of this gratification, often employ political rhetoric justifying their actions on moral grounds, even though these grounds are usually outrageous, not-too-hidden assumptions, such as the assumption that one particular racial strain is superior to all others. For even the worst demagogues and tyrants feel a need for at least the trappings of moral justification, the need for rationalizing the irrational, the convenient, or the profitable.

Confucius and even his inscrutable and mystic predecessor, Lao Tzu, also were involved in training philosophical leaders, and in teaching leaders philosophy. Confucius aimed his very insightful instruction at the creation of what could be translated today as "great person." The undesirable opposite of this ideal he labeled "petty person." One of the main questions asked time and again in *The Sayings of Confucius* is whether a particular leader should be called "great" or "petty." For example, a leader who put personal considerations above moral obligations would definitely be seen as "petty." Confucius also used the terms for his students. As a matter of fact you could say it was his way of grading his students; i.e., "great" stood for "A;" "petty" for "F." Lao Tzu's approach was an advanced calculus of wisdom in comparison to Confucius' moral algebra, but he also ranked his leaders according to their practice of higher wisdom, the wisdom of being one with what he perceived as the *tao,* or way, of the universe. For both, ideal leaders exemplified in their lives the government most highly desired in their domains.

Students reading Plato, Confucius, and Lao Tzu can benefit most by applying, *mainly to themselves,* the principles that these famous thinkers of antiquity expounded, and only secondarily by using them for comparative analysis of world leaders. That is, what originally was written and taught for a handful of future leaders and bureaucrats can now become the democratic property and inspiration of many. I believe that this is not a perversion of the original intention, but instead an excellent extending of that intention to the only "leaders" capable of forming a viable, just, and truly successful government—individual people themselves.

*For is not self-government the basis of good government?* Hobbes suggested that without a strong, authoritative, and vigilantly-imposed government we would find ourselves at the mercy of everyone's worse instincts. This is true in so far as people cannot or will not govern their worse instincts. But it is also false in so far as each individual is able and willing to practice self-government.

The formula is obvious: *the less self-government people are willing to impose upon themselves, individual by individual, family by family, social group by social group, community by community, business by business, and at all the other levels of possible self-regulation, the more government control people must be subjected to,* the more invasion of privacy they invite, and the more likely they are to find themselves largely under the control of a massive bureaucracy that claims to be democratic, or communistic, or of whatever political persuasion currently and locally has the most popular appeal, but is in reality virtually totalitarian.

Therefore, we come back once more to *the individual*—not to an individual practicing unrestricted freedom, which is not freedom at all but license, and which is one of the most direct roads to Hobbesian authoritarianism; but to the individual developing *the higher freedom of self-government*, a freedom from the tyranny of our worst weaknesses—arrogance, anger, lust, intemperance, selfishness, laziness, dishonesty, and cowardice.

The more you develop the freedom of self-government, the more you will be in control of what happens in your life, and the less you will be pushed around by every whim and desire that develops within you or is suggested by your friends or by those in your society who profit by your lack of self-control. The college student who can go to Saturday night parties and not drink at all, or at least, not drink too much; the teenager in the inner-city who can avoid or resist the drug scene; the employee in a company who is willing to risk being fired rather than pretend not to notice unfair, dishonest, or harmful business practices; the executive who makes humanitarian and ecological issues an integral part of decision-making—all these individuals are practicing the freedom of self-government.

I once devoted three sections of a research-paper class to an extensive investigation of the world's wisdom literature, the type of philosophy most worth studying as far as I am concerned. The amazing result was that almost all of the writers consulted, from ancient times to the present, found the greatest happiness available to the individual to be self-government! They, however, used an older word to describe this freedom. The word was "virtue." The word itself, for those who believe that virtue is only for milksops, means "manliness" and implies the strength, discipline, courage, and determination needed to develop this freedom within you. Today, I would suggest the term be translated as "humanliness," since virtue is essential to *all* of us, male *and* female.

Being a barbarian who gives free rein to any of humankind's worst instincts is not being a man, it is not being a woman, it is being a menace to yourself and others, and an open invitation for the strictest version of Hobbesian government possible.

The state trooper stopping you for drunken driving, or the police officer crashing through your door on a drug bust, is on the scene by your invitation. For *the more you can't govern yourself, the more you ask others to govern you.* But the best proof of anything is to be found in trying it.

Pick one of your "petty" behaviors and work on controlling it. It may take a long time to make headway since the behavior in one form or another has probably been with you for quite a while. However, I guarantee you'll eventually appreciate and enjoy being in control of this behavior rather than being controlled by it.

When I was quite young, I had—perhaps because of serious family problems I did not understand, and perhaps for genetic reasons, or some slight chemical imbalance in my brain, or for all these reasons and more—a terrible, seemingly uncontrollable temper. A

Vesuvius of emotion would erupt and overwhelm the Pompeii of my entire being. In a temper tantrum 1 would throw anything at hand at my playmates, and one time I almost strangled my best friend. Moreover, I frightened myself, for I would act like one possessed. Over many years I have gradually—very gradually—worked my way to *A SUCCESSFUL CONTROL OF THAT WHICH USED TO CONTROL ME.* But it took time, work, and determination. It took learning to be more aware of circumstances that might lead to and symptoms indicating a potential episode. It took learning how to be assertive by expressing my feelings (rather than suppressing them) in order to avoid the build up of stress and tension that usually would precede my loss of emotional control. However, the victory was well worth the struggle. The self-government of my temper, despite occasional rumblings and small explosions, has been a blessing both to myself and to others, especially to my wife and our children.

**\*\*\*\***

The more of us who improve our self-government, the better; for *in modern times what we need more than philosopher rulers are philosopher citizens,* citizens willing to earn the freedom and happiness of self-government. With enough of these citizens around we will have less need for ever-increasing government control and may eventually even get more versions of Plato's philosopher leader and fewer versions of Confucius' "petty" leader.

The *way* awaits.

The *choice* is yours.

Before you criticize the chaos your government is in, be sure you've got your own self-government in good shape.

To paraphrase J. F. K.,
"ASK NOT WHAT YOUR GOVERNMENT CAN DO FOR YOU, BUT WHAT YOU CAN DO FOR YOUR OWN SELF-GOVERNMENT."

*Before you expect anything of others, expect it of yourself.*

BE YOUR OWN PHILOSOPHER RULER.

Or as Confucius (would) say, referring not to fame but to character,
"BE GREAT PERSON."

*Clay Boland Jr.*

# SECTION V: MAKING THE MOST OF IT

*Clay Boland Jr.*

## WORKING AND LIVING

> *"It seems that we can develop a kind of philosophy which enables us to gain some distinction or knowledge but does not enable us to cope with the daily issues of living. Many well-informed persons are in a constant state of inner agitation and fail to enjoy inner happiness and peace. The most important thing has not been learned—*
> *HOW TO CONDUCT OURSELVES*
> *SO THAT WE MAY*
> *TRULY LIVE."*
> *—Alfred Montapert*

We make a great mistake in separating working and living. *Unless we are willing to put more living into our work and more work into our living, neither will give us the satisfaction it should.* As it is, we put the two in distinct categories and pretend that they have nothing to do with each other. We then exacerbate the situation by preparing intently for one and almost totally neglecting preparation for the other. The same is true of our "maintenance" of both—one gets a lot, the other a little.

And to insure that the next generation finds itself in the same predicament, we support an educational system that reflects our "lopsided" thinking.

133

The increasing emphasis on career training at the expense of education for living is causing more and more personal problems in our society, problems that bring about loneliness, alienation, and "emptiness" in our lives. We are urged from an early age to devote our main energies to preparing for a career and becoming professional or expert in a particular line of work, but *when it comes to the larger work of living fulfilled and meaningful lives in a confusing world, we are more or less left on our own to muddle through in whatever amateur fashion we can.*

And so, although it is no trouble for most of us to succeed in our jobs, most of us struggle on and on, having setback after setback as we try to succeed in our lives. And, as a result, our ability to help others, including our friends, relatives, brothers, sisters, and children, succeed in their lives is often equally unsuccessful.

To succeed in our careers at the expense of our lives is both costly and tragic.

To succeed in neither is even worse.

THERE IS NO REASON NOT TO SUCCEED IN *BOTH.*

# ART AND EXISTENCE

I would ask you to consider looking at your life as a "work of art." I would ask you to think of your individual existence as a human, kind or unkind, and your existence as part of humankind, or "humanunkind," as an artistic endeavor, as a work of art continually in progress. This does not imply that you are in the process of creating a masterpiece with your life—most of us are bound to be falling far short of that—but that the same *influences* and *dynamics* that are involved in the creation of a work of art, no matter how good or how bad, are involved in the "creation" of the "art work" called your life. And I would ask you to consider, as a corollary, that the "art work" called your life, in turn, influences many other "art works"; i.e., many other lives.

Do not almost all human activities involve art, and are we not all artists? Just as the composer works with the "raw material" of sound, shaping its elements into a content that communicates, we too shape our lives and thereby artistically create "compositions" we listen to and perform for others every day of our lives.

Fortunately, we can keep revising, altering, dropping and adding sections, introducing new themes or touching up old ones, changing the mood created by altering a multitude of variables, getting help from fellow artists, and so forth. The analogy can be made with any of the traditionally recognized art forms.

Just about everything we do involves artistic skills. For instance, the quality of our appreciation and the keenness of our perception of the world around us depend on how well we have developed our ability to observe, rather than just to see; our ability to listen, rather than just to hear; our ability to discern fine distinctions, rather than just indifferently taste, smell, and feel; our ability to "read" our own body language and that of others, rather than hardly notice it; and our ability to interpret emotional and personal "climates" and "sensibilities," rather than ignore them.

Furthermore, drawing on the theatrical arts for a moment, the way we present ourselves to the "audience" of the world as players on the stage of life depends largely on artistic judgments and decisions that we make ourselves—or let others make for us. The way we dress, groom, walk, talk, sit, and stand; the maintenance of or disregard for our physical fitness and health; the subjects we show interest in and like to discuss; the careers we pursue; the hobbies, activities, and sports we prefer; the friends we spend our time with; the books and magazines and newspapers we read; the kind of music we listen to; our living accommodations; the way we approach our work; the way we spend our leisure time; the way we make love; the way we share love; the way we withhold love; the way we treat others; the wisdom we follow in our lives; the wisdom we ignore; the character strengths and weaknesses we cultivate; the priorities we live by; the goals we set for ourselves—all of these are partially the results of artistic judgments and decisions we make about the components of the individual "work of art" called a "human being" that each one of us creates out of the materials we have to work with.

And all of these, in turn, are also partially the results of *all* the artistic *influences* that are constantly working on and modifying that individual "work of art" each one of us creates. It is therefore up to you individually, as a card-carrying member of "us," to *choose your influences carefully,* and not just allow yourself to be influenced by whatever set of influences you happen to find most accessible in your particular "environment." Let's take, to demonstrate the point, the influence of two arts: interior decorating and music.

Either, like every art, can be used to inspire us, to uplift us, to encourage us; or, on the other hand, to sap our resolve, to dehumanize us, and to hinder our daily efforts to be affirmative and congenial. Either can also, like every art, lead us to positive or negative thoughts. Either can make us mindful, or render us mindless. Either can act on us in many other *less* dramatic ways, but these polarities should suffice to make the point.

In your involvement with either—as in your selection of reading materials, television programs, movies, and so forth—in all the *choices* you make about each "art" that will influence you (or that you don't make and allow others to make for you), *you "shape" yourself or allow yourself to be "shaped."* And if you are willing to entertain the idea that all of us are "works of art," then you can add to the list all your friends, acquaintances, neighbors, and everyone else in your life, and even those that you consciously or unconsciously choose as role models from afar, in the past or in the present—the heroes and heroines of your personal mythology.

To start with, consider the ambience in a college cafeteria. Everything in this ambience, as just about everything around you that has been produced by people, has been fashioned with some level, no matter how elementary, of artistic skill, judgment, and deliberation.

If you happen to be a college student at a prestigious university, and as usual are having lunch in an oak-paneled, brass-chandeliered, three-story-high dining room with large picture windows overlooking the botanical gardens, and are sitting at a table with a tablecloth, linen napkins, and a floral display freshly picked for the day; you are being influenced by an ambience of *elegance,* which in turn makes you feel elegant and increases your self-esteem.

If you happen to be a college student at a local community college, and as usual are having lunch in an antiseptic, low-ceiling, garishly-lit-with-fluorescent-lights dining room with a splendid view of the parking lot, and are sitting at a folding, light green, linoleum-covered, slightly unstable, multi-purpose, food-stained and penknife-initialed table with no table cloth, paper napkins that you brought to the table yourself, and a display of crumbled styrofoam cups and plates strewn here and there for your aesthetic pleasure; you are being influenced by an ambience of *shoddiness,* which in turn makes you feel shoddy and decreases your self-esteem.

In both cases, you will probably complain about the food (since that is a favorite topic of conversation in all college dining rooms). And in the second case, you can, of course, rise above the influence of the interior decorating by supplying good friendship and interesting conversation in compensation. Nonetheless, you are being negatively influenced, and must make an effort to "transcend" your given environment. And in both cases, the vocabulary and grammar used, the kinds of subjects discussed, and the intelligence revealed by the students at the table are also creating an ambience, an artistic influence.

The inescapable fact is that almost anywhere you go, while you are doing almost anything you can think of, you are constantly being bombarded by art, and it is therefore important that you understand what interior decorating, music, or any other art form acting on you is communicating. It is important, as well, to understand *what* its "magic" or power is, or at least to understand *how* its "magic" or power can radically affect you.

To convince yourself of the very powerful artistic influence of the "ambience" we call music, turn on your radio and spend some time listening to all the music stations that you usually *don't* listen to. As you listen, try to get a feeling for how the music is "working on" you, for what effect it is having on your emotions, for what kind of mood and "headset" it is creating. Then extend your initial reactions by imagining how listening to each particular type of music over a long period of time would modify your personality. Similar experiments can be done with colors and the moods they evoke, or with languages and language usage and the views of life they encourage in their speakers.

As you become more and more aware of the influence of "art" in your life, *it is obviously to your advantage to choose those artistic influences that are beneficial—and equally to your advantage to avoid harmful ones.*

I have often invited my students to try the following "psycho-musical" experiment (but so far have had no takers—which may be excellent proof of the average college student's sanity). I have invited them to either spend two weeks listening to nothing but the symphonies and concerti of Ludwig Von Beethoven, or to spend two weeks listening to nothing but the most radical works of Igor Stravinsky, such as his *Rite of Spring.* I am sure that the personality changes undergone would be very interesting, for these two different "brands" of music would bring about a change (whether temporary or permanent I can't say) in the way the "test" listeners would feel about themselves and the world.

Confucius put it well when he said, "Let me hear the music of a province, and I will tell you what kind of people live there." I'd add, along the same lines, let me know the music you listen to and love, and I'll have a fairly good idea about what kind of person you are. And, if you're not happy with the kind of person you are, for openers, why not change your tunes?

Why not change *any* artistic influences that are "shaping" you in a way that you don't like. It's your right to do so. It's your life to live. It's your art work.

As in all things, *there is much more that you can do to improve your life than you might think possible.* Although you are not only daily shaping yourself as a "work of art," and are also, even if you are unaware or unwilling to care, being shaped by all the "works of art" around you,

## YOU HAVE A LOT MORE
## ARTISTIC CONTROL OF YOUR LIFE
## THAN YOU PROBABLY REALIZE.

*The question is how much responsibility you wish to take for being in charge of the art work called your life, and how much responsibility you wish to delegate by allowing others and their art to control you.*

Whether the present version of "the art work called your life" is pleasing to you or otherwise, it is an artistic consolation to know that, *with whatever materials you have been given,* you have either done the best that you could do (or close to it), or that you have the artistic freedom to do better.

The worst version of the situation—creating a "work of art" that nobody, including the creator, wishes to behold—can be found in Oscar Wilde's *Picture of Dorian Gray.* Dorian Gray, as a young man, has his portrait painted. Everyone remarks on the exact resemblance and on the extraordinary handsomeness of the sitter. But a very strange thing happens. As Dorian Gray immerses himself in a life of self-indulgence and brings about the downfall and destruction of those he "uses" for his own pleasure and gain, the portrait begins to change. The once handsome face starts to show signs of depravity, dissipation, and viciousness; and yet Dorian himself continues to appear just as he did in his portrait. Not wanting anyone to see these telltale signs that are beginning to appear on the face in his portrait, but not on his own face, he puts his portrait in an upstairs room to which only he has the key.

As his Hogarthian *Rake's Progress* continues, the face in his portrait "develops" a sickly complexion, ugly sags, ulcerous lesions, tumorous warts, and a permanent, snarling leer. Dorian, however, still looks as handsome as ever. His visits to the upstairs room become less and less frequent. He is more and more unwilling to face the "monster" he has "created."

Finally, in remorse, shame, and disgust, he ascends to his private upstairs room, and in hatred of his "work of art" slashes through it with a knife in order to destroy it. His servants, having heard a cry and a loud crash, enter the upstairs room from the roof and find the dead body of a repulsively ugly ogre with a knife in his chest. On the wall there hangs the original, unaltered, undisturbed portrait of Dorian Gray as a handsome young man. It is only by the rings on his hands that they recognize that the ogre is Dorian Gray himself.

Interestingly enough, Oscar Wilde was drawing, for his 1891 Victorian allegory, on the well-known fact that the way we live our lives gradually begins to show in our faces, in our postures, in the sound of our voices, and in all the wealth of evidence we offer to others. We can only be thankful that there are not too many active and observant "life-as-an-art-form" critics among us, for we can't hide ourselves in an upstairs room but are forced by necessity to go about our business. The answer to the dilemma, of course, is to try to live in such a way that our "portraits" are ones that we, as well as others, like to look at.

\*\*\*\*

*The greatest art of all is the art of life, for it is not only the most challenging of all the arts, but it is also the only art available to each and every one of us. To make of our individual lives the outstanding "works of art" they can be, and to make of our brief sojourns in this world with others the "works of art" they should be, are artistic endeavors available to one and all.*

The better we become as artists in these important artistic endeavors, the better for every one, for *THE ARTS OF INDIVIDUAL LIFE AND LIVING WITH OTHERS ARE THE ARTS THAT DETERMINE THE QUALITY OF OUR MUTUAL EXISTENCE.*

These arts are available to all, and yet a vast majority of people believe that they are victims of their circumstances rather than the shapers of their opportunities, that they are just characters in the novels of their lives rather than the novelists, just dancers in the ballets of their lives rather than the choreographers, just members of the orchestra rather than the composers who "call the tunes."

Ah, but you say, "Art is all very fine to talk about, but in practice nature turns out to be a very difficult 'medium' to work in and work with!" Whether you believe that there *is* such a thing as "human nature," a nature possessing predictable propensities for both good and bad, or whether such an idea is repulsive to you, it would still be a folly—unless scientists of the future can alter the situation—to expect that any *modus operandi* of nature, such as the sexual drive or the instinct for survival, can change or be changed to any great extent.

Nor can most individuals hope to dramatically change any of the genetically-inherited neurological, physiological, and physical handicaps they were born with. These are part of the "givens"—as are the effects of early childhood traumas, disappointments, and tribulations that all of us must deal with since all of us have them. And as if that weren't enough, a number of us have other problems caused by accidents and diseases, and even by alcohol and drug abuse, which in turn lengthen the list of "givens" with which we must work.

However, that being the way things are, does not mean that there is nothing that can be done about "the human predicament." The wisest thing to do is to ACCEPT THE "GIVENS" AND CREATE THE BEST RESULTS POSSIBLE OUT OF THEM. Nevertheless, many people go through their lives refusing to "accept the givens," *especially the ones they don't like or find inconvenient,* and an equal number decide early in their lives that it is just too much work to "create the best results possible out of them."

It might help, since we are talking about artists and art, to consider yourself, for the sake of inspiration, as Michelangelo, and your unique version of "nature" as the large block of marble, nicknamed "The Giant," that so many had been unable to do anything with before him. That gigantic block of marble had been "flawed" by an earlier sculptor, but Michelangelo triumphed over the Goliath of a rock and its "original" flaw to create a symbol for all times—a symbol of the potential of humankind—his "David."

Working with this particular "given," he worked slowly and patiently until he "found" within the block, within the almost shapeless chaos of *seemingly* unworkable and unyielding substance, the beauty that was "locked" within. Did he complain that the marble was too hard? Perhaps, but he kept on working because he had a "vision" of what he could create out of it. Did he complain that the task was too difficult, that too much patience and thought were called for? Perhaps, but I doubt it, for he was well aware of the demands of his favorite art, sculpture. The exhilaration of meeting the challenge is what drove him on. The beauty he was in the process of creating, and finally did create, was his reward—a beauty that has inspired millions of people ever since.

Yes, "nature" is a difficult medium to work in and work with, but learn to bring to it *patience,* learn to bring to it *the willingness to work with obdurant and flawed material.* Accept, or better than that, learn to love the "given" and *to find exhilaration in making the best you can out of it.*

Find the best "artistic influences" you can and let them help you in your artistic endeavors—you will need the strength, inspiration, and insights they can give you. Apply what you learn from them.

*You don't have to be a genius to succeed; nor do you need to be famous to be considered a success.*

Best of all, in "the arts of individual life and living with others," the success of one adds to the success of all. These are the arts of the world's oldest and best "grassroots movement." These are the arts we can all practice.

Study what others have done and are doing.

Learn the skills.

Learn the principles.

Train yourself.

Practice daily.

Become the best artist you can be.

\*\*\*\*

Whatever other forms of immortality may exist, including the "immortality" of bringing children into the world to "continue our lives" for us, we can all gain immortality, as Norman Cousins has suggested in his book, *The Celebration of Life,* by the influence of our lives on others, for that influence in one form or another "lives on and on."

I recall a hot summer evening long ago when I was "down and out" in New York City, feeling blue and almost suicidal. I went to dinner at the same local, inexpensive, and fairly shoddy cafeteria at which I had had my last five hundred meals, since it was close to where I was living, and since I had no cooking facilities in my very small West Side rented room. As I was standing in line to get some mashed potatoes and chicken, the young woman busily working at the steam table took the time to give me a pleasant smile while she asked me what I wanted. I have often thought that simple gesture saved my life. It immediately changed my mood and put me back in touch with the human race. I should mention that the policy of the cafeteria was to hire ex-convicts as employees, for I want you to know that her ability to smile at anyone was earned the hard way.

Yes, the "art" of our lives influences others every moment of our lives, and will continue to influence others who are yet to be born after we die. Our *every action,* our *every word,* and even our *every thought* can each be compared to a pebble tossed onto the surface of a mountain pond, its ripples circling wider and wider, its waves traveling further and further.

And so, I would like to pass that "smile" on to you, and with it make you feel better, and with it put you back in touch with the human race, and with it encourage you—with whatever materials you have been given—to

HELP YOURSELF
AND ALL OF US
BY BEING
THE BEST ARTIST
YOU
CAN
BE.

# THERE IS NO GOODBYE

THERE IS NO GOODBYE.

THERE IS NO DEATH.

WE LIVE ON IN EACH OTHER

AND IN OTHERS YET TO BE.

## ETHICAL ILLUSIONS

It is unrealistic and unreasonable to expect people to be *perfect,* and yet most of us do. Many ethical systems, religious doctrines, and utopian depictions of ideal societies encourage us to think we should be—and even could be—perfect. One only needs to reread the "Sermon in the Mount" to understand why Shaw quipped that "the last Christian died on the cross." No one, except Jesus, has ever been able to live up to all of its advice. And even Jesus preferred the company of the disreputable to that of the Pharisees.

For those who see counsels of perfection as goals that can't be reached, but goals that are worth striving for nevertheless, these counsels are usually helpful. But for those who believe that they are actually attainable, and who castigate themselves and others on a daily basis for failure to live up to them, these counsels can often be more *harmful* than helpful. In some cases, the strain of trying to be perfect results in temporary or permanent escapes into saturnalias of imperfection. H. L. Mencken suggested a parallel to this when he pointed out that the nations most repressed in peace are the ones most zealous in war.

It may be more realistic and reasonable to admit that we are all imperfect, to admit that there is much that is not admirable in every one of us. But we can balance this admission by being thankful that most of us most of the time manage to be *less imperfect* than we can be, and that there is much that is admirable in every one of us. In Interpersonal Communications classes, students often find it difficult to say good things about themselves. However, they are never at a loss for words when talking about their failings and the failings of those close to them. *But why should we not praise the good in ourselves and others?* Why do we constantly harp on that which *isn't* good in ourselves and others? We have given criticism itself a bad name. Its original function was to divide the good from the bad. We, however, generally concentrate our efforts in regard to ourselves and others on the negative and totally neglect the positive.

The next time you start to criticize yourself or someone else, READ THE ETHICAL ILLUSION IN REVERSE. Just as an optical illusion can be seen in more than one way, so can the *complete* picture of a person's ethical behavior be seen in more than one way.

Rather than frustrating yourself with trying to be perfect, and rather than being constantly surprised at and dissatisfied with yourself and everyone else for not being as perfect as you would wish, *compliment yourself and others for being less imperfect than either you or they can be.*

****

*Perhaps one of our greatest imperfections is expecting ourselves and others to be perfect.*

*Perhaps one of our greatest perfections is accepting our own and others' imperfections, and applauding anyone's ability to rise above them.*

If you haven't learned to forgive yourself or somebody near to you, then you probably haven't internalized this.

For you, Achilles will always be found wanting. He will always be a heel.

For you, the good that those near to you do will be "interred with their bones."

For you, the ethical illusion will always appear with its dark shapes in the foreground and its light shapes, if noticeable at all, in the background.

# LIVING WITH ONE FOOT IN THE GRAVE OF THE PAST

THE PAST,
YOU YESTERDAY—
DEAD, CHISELLED-GRANITE DEAD.

THE PRESENT,
YOU TODAY—
ALIVE, GROWING-GREEN-GRASS ALIVE!

IF YOU REFUSED TO EXPERIENCE IT THEN,
DO SO NOW
AND BE DONE WITH IT.
How?
BY DOING IT!

IF YOU HAVEN'T FORGIVEN YOURSELF
OR SOMEONE ELSE,
DO SO NOW
AND BE DONE WITH IT.
How?
BY DOING IT!

IF OPPORTUNITIES WERE MISSED THEN,
THERE ARE OTHER OPPORTUNITIES NOW,
AND THEY MIGHT EVEN BE BETTER.

IF EVERYTHING WENT WRONG THEN,
YOU DON'T HAVE TO LET THE FACT
MAKE EVERYTHING GO WRONG NOW.

LEARN FROM YOUR PAST FAILURES,
WITHOUT REGRET;
LEARN FROM YOUR PAST SUCCESSES,
WITHOUT REGRET;
AND GET ON WITH YOUR LIFE.

DON'T LIVE WITH ONE FOOT IN THE GRAVE OF THE
PAST;
LIVE WITH BOTH FEET PLANTED FIRMLY ON THE
SOLID,
FLOWER-COVERED *TERRA FIRMA*
OF THE
PRESENT.

TO BE HALF DEAD IS
TO BE ONLY HALF ALIVE.

# PRIORITIES

*Life is complicated and problematic enough without the additional complications and problems we ourselves add to it.* Instead of balancing three balls in the air, which is hard enough, most of us seem to insist on trying to juggle eight or nine or ten. Then we wonder why we're having trouble keeping most of them from falling to the ground.

For example, take our confusion about what is important. Without a clear-cut idea of what is of more importance and what is of less importance in any given situation, we are constantly worrying about the validity and benefit of what we are doing. We become periodically paralyzed by self-induced and needless emotional turmoil and mental torture about even the most insignificant decisions. As a result, we are often unable to make major decisions as well and unable to enjoy for very long anything we do because we keep thinking we are doing the wrong thing—and therefore should be doing something else. We do not need to punish ourselves this way. Frenzy is not an optimal state of being. Such frantic behavior causes brain ulcers. The only people who profit from it are in the drug, alcohol, and nonstop-distraction businesses, since most of us only seem to have the time for short-term palliatives rather than for long-term cures.

If any of these symptoms are ones from which you suffer, I would like to offer you a long-term cure by helping you to understand one of their main causes—

the absence of *conscious, beneficial, nonconflicting, realistic, and hierarchical priorities* in your life.

Of course, *you already have priorities in your life, but you probably are not quite sure what they are.* Your priorities may be more or less unidentified, or even "hidden," because there may be some you don't want to let yourself know about. Nevertheless, other people, looking at your life more objectively, may easily recognize what you yourself are unaware of or don't want to admit. How do they know? By your choices and conversation and behavior. So, if you wish to get a fairly accurate idea of what your present priorities are, you could ask a good friend to list them for you. But it might be safer to make the effort to detect them yourself first before comparing notes with someone else. Be your own Sherlock Holmes and look at the evidence. Look at your daily choices, at the time you devote to various activities, at the subjects you find yourself thinking and talking about the most, and at the typical behaviors that you predictably bring to various situations, especially to difficult ones. Then, by inductive reasoning, add the clues together, and with a very British, "Elementary, my dear Watson," you should be able to clearly state what your priorities really are.

Let's imagine for a moment that your investigation reveals that both the "murdered" and the "murderer" are one and the same, that your "hidden agenda" of priorities is a fairly self-destructive one, including some or all of the following items: "to feel sorry for yourself," "to think about eating, drinking, or 'getting laid' all the time," "to do as little work as possible," "to party as much as possible," "to avoid responsibility as long as you can," "to go through the motions in everything you do but to only get involved now and then," "to *get* as much as you can and *give* as little as you can," "to be passive and apathetic," "to blame everybody and everything else but yourself for all your problems, bad luck, and hardships," and so forth.

When you have put together your list of present priorities, it would, therefore, be wise to first *determine if everything on your list of recently discovered priorities is beneficial.* There may be some items on the list, such as the ones listed in the hypothetical case given above, that represent tickets to nowhere or to even less desirable destinations. There may be some items that offer short-term gains but long-term pains. There may be certain items that are inspired by resentment, or by a desire for revenge, or by what you perceive as a need for punishing yourself. All of these items and any like them that are equally detrimental should be replaced with healthier alternatives. And if you need help to replace them, get it. If it's free, don't discount it as of no value. If it costs money that you don't want to spend, you may be making a choice between "your money or your life" if you don't spend it.

Next, it will be interesting to *observe whether some of your priorities actually conflict with others.* Let's say that "to be popular with members of the opposite sex" is a big priority on your list, but at the same time "to act like a total loser" is also a big item because you enjoy the attention it gains for you. The outcome of this conflict of priorities is too painful to spell out. An effective way of "cleaning up your act," then, would be removing conflicts from your "hidden agenda."

In establishing a revised list of priorities, it helps to *pick priorities that are* not only beneficial and nonconflicting but also *realistic.* I believe the kind of *priorities that are available to all people at all times in their lives are the most realistic* simply because anyone can realistically hope to achieve the goals that they represent at any time of life. Such priorities would be "to be more positive," "to stop shortchanging yourself and your abilities," "to talk less and listen more," "to develop your potential more fully in an area of personal aptitude and interest," "to make yourself more interesting," "to be more independent," "to be less selfish," "to be more outgoing," and so on.

Priorities such as "to have a 'fantabulous' sex life," "to be a celebrity," "to always be the center of attention," "to do just as you wish," "to be wealthy," and others of the same nature are unrealistic for most people and therefore the cause of much misery for those who become committed to them as the *only* possible sources of happiness. And they also can easily become sources of frustration and sadness for other people in your life. Don't make the mistake of putting them high on your list. It might even be smarter not to put them on your list at all. Although they may seem glamorous, they are fool's gold, and you prospect for them at the risk of isolating yourself from the rest of us.

Becoming famous or wealthy, for example, in most cases takes outstanding natural aptitude, incredible persistence, plenty of hard and unending work day after day after day, the right connections, the right circumstances, being in the right place at the right time, and lots and lots of luck. If you have made a realistic assessment of yourself in comparison to those who are successful in the career you wish to pursue, go for it if you wish. Work at it diligently, give it your "blood, sweat, and tears," but don't pin all your hopes on the results—they will happen or they won't. And whatever you do, don't cut yourself off from everyone else in the process. On the way to something only a handful of people achieve, *you still need to live, and with the right priorities your life can be rewarding while you're getting there or not getting there.*

With the right priorities, in the most significant sense, *you'll already be there.* You'll already be demonstrating that you understand the wisdom of that well-known saying: "The journey is the destination." You'll already have the satisfactions others struggle for fame and wealth to have, only in many cases discovering to their regret that while achieving their goals they have lost on the way what they hoped their goals would give them.

The next thing to do is to *rank your priorities so that one is more important than all the others,* and so that all the others follow it in order of their importance. Actually the word "priorities" indicates something that can't exist—a number of "first choices." However, through usage the word has come to mean those goals that are the ones you believe to be the most important. Therefore, it is necessary to rank your priorities so that if you are forced to make a choice between two of them, you can choose the higher-ranking one.

Finally, I would suggest keeping the list short, and even, if you wish to insure a good rate of success, limiting it to *one* item. That one item will then return you to the original meaning of "priority," "a first choice," and simplify the job of implementing it. If you later wish to extend the list and add second and third choices, or more, fine. But first, try just *one: numero uno.*

Let's say, for instance, that your priority is to maintain equanimity; i.e., equal-spiritedness or calmness. When faced with a decision, you can then ask yourself, "Would plan A or plan B be more conducive to maintaining equanimity?" Then you can choose accordingly. If you find you've made the wrong choice, in most cases you can still decide to react calmly, rather than frantically. You can still choose, despite the circumstances, to achieve your priority of maintaining your equanimity.

In any situation in which you find your peace of mind dissipating, stop and check what you are doing to add to this loss of equanimity. Also check what you can do to regain your composure.

Remember, as well, that a decision is a "cutting off" *(de,* from; *cision,* as in incision, a cutting). Therefore, to achieve your priority may mean not achieving other desired goals, or only achieving them to a lesser degree. In a discussion with someone whose views are completely in opposition to your own, you may decide that shouting your opponent down might be great fun, but that it's more important to keep your calm by not taking yourself or your opponent too seriously.

And to insure ongoing success with your priority, remind yourself of it in the morning when you're dressing and throughout the day. Keep it in mind and let it do its good work of keeping you "together."

Choose a good *"numero uno"* and stay with it one day at a time.

And one day at a time, watch the complications and problems diminish.

## ENJOYING LIFE

> *"Joy can be sweet. Or it can be zesty, euphoric, giddy. It can teach. It can heal. It can lay to rest old pain. In a world...darkened by suffering and uncertainty, joy can brighten our heavens and make life worth living again."*
> —*Philip Kunhardt Jr.*

*Sunday morning, early August, 1990. Home Valley, Washington. Walking through fields near the Columbia River Gorge.*

I had a most pleasant thought this morning while I was walking our half-Golden Retriever, half-Great Pyrenees, Sam, after having set up my wife at the windsurfing beach and having set out to take Sam for some exercise before joining her there—today, I'm going to enjoy life.

Now most people who know me believe that I do, and the fact is I do much of the time, but almost as often I also suffer—due to bad attitude, false expectations, what I perceive as unfulfilled desires, and so on through the list of self-created tortures we are so good at wishing on ourselves. Today, however, my priority is to enjoy myself.

Sam bounces along with that felicitous ease and grace which all animals possess and which most humans seem to have lost—but which we would all do well to emulate more often in our lives—following his wonderfully keen nose here, there, and back again, thoroughly enjoying our outing.

As we meander through the beautiful Skamania County Home Valley Park, I vicariously enjoy the Mozartian effortlessness and Phidian fluidity with which he moves.

I admire the rapidly moving water and the views of cathedrals of cliff and lush green hills rising from the river on the Oregon side. In particular, recalling Joyce Kilmer's famous lines, I stop to "read" the ancient deciduous and evergreen "poems" left standing here and there throughout the park (some of which must date back to the days when Lewis and Clark explored this very same terrain), each one a magnificent example of the grand "art" of nature. Van Gogh can capture our imaginations, our emotions, and our appreciation by his recreation of a somber, dark green cypress tree or of a vase of bright yellow sunflowers, but how much more exquisite is the original—nature in all its beauty (and all the more beautiful because it is both timeless and ephemeral, constant in its themes but constantly working variations on those themes, changing as it does in subtle ways from day to day and even while we observe it).

As we pass by an opening in the trees that allows us a river vista, I can see below us the sunlit, colorful butterfly wings (half a pair for each windsurfing board) skimming quickly and quietly back and forth over the whitecapped swells covering the broad Columbia River, which happens to be majestically wide at this particular location.

Naturally, I want to be out there skimming back and forth myself, and soon I will be. But wait—now

I'm spending time walking with Sam and communing with nature, and I am *not* out there on the river. So, if I am to enjoy life, it is crucial to get what I can from what is happening rather than what will be happening or what I would like to be happening.

Sam rolls over on his back and writhes about, delighting in a self-created back-scratching on the grass. I kneel down and rub his chest and give him a good massage under his chin. If he could purr, he would. As it is, he manages to open his lips slightly, revealing his very small lower teeth to indicate a mild state of canine ecstasy. If I am impatient to move on to the windsurfing beach, rig up a sail, and get out "where the action is," this moment will be meaningless and lost for me. So I enjoy it—by which I mean I *fully* live it.

I cannot help but think of those who have jobs they don't or won't enjoy, jobs they simply "survive," that they simply "get through," day after day after day. I also recall a number of people with menial and boring jobs who have decided to make them interesting and meaningful—a young check-out clerk at a Safeway supermarket in The Dalles comes to mind, for she tries to interact with all her customers, making her day and theirs just a little bit better.

Sam finds a rotting piece of discarded steak fat, which he deems worthy of vigorously rubbing both sides of his head into in order to carry valuable information back to the pack his long, long ago ancestors belonged to.

Then, unbidden, my mind starts its own pleasurable activity—searching through the materials it has collected over the years, and finding interesting items I am inspired to rub both sides of my brain against.

For some reason, perhaps because the thought of enjoying life is considered almost sinful by some people and was especially considered so by earlier generations of Americans, as exemplified by the dour, joyless couple in Grant Wood's "American Gothic," the idea of suffering comes to mind, and then its geometrical symbol, the cruciform—a long vertical crossed by a short horizontal about three-quarters of the way to the top.

This symbol, which conveys the main religious "message" behind Western Civilization, says that life is suffering, and here I am saying that I will enjoy life.

Am I being sacrilegious? Or, perhaps, would I be more sacrilegious if I were to depreciate the wonderful gifts of life and the beauties of nature by not enjoying them, or by enjoying them less than I could?

And the long vertical—what does that "register" in my psyche or in the "collective unconscious" Carl Jung has suggested that we all share? The lower, and longer, part of the vertical—our bodies, growing from or attached to the earth as it were and which therefore are subject to deterioration, which also often "drag us down" by fighting against our better inclinations?

The short, and higher, part of the vertical—the human spirit, the source of those higher goals which are so hard to reach, but are always worth striving for?

The horizontal—the stretch and pull of the world and natural processes on the unity and upward aspirations that all individuals, all groups of people, all nations find so difficult to fulfill?

And what are our higher aspirations? A heaven? A better world?

But what about both—*now*? What about heaven here on earth? Is this also a profane idea? Or is waiting for death in order to enjoy life an equally or *more* profane idea?

Whatever the answer, heaven here on earth is an unlikely prospect. There are enough people among us who are determined to make sure it doesn't happen for anybody—including themselves—to prevent it from coming about. And even without such people around, suffering would still remain part of life because it's inescapable.

I do think, nonetheless, that we can create *some* heaven right here for ourselves and for others by making the most of our potential and energy, and by taking the time to appreciate the good things that are always available to us.

Nobody can deny that suffering is a part of life, but so is enjoyment. *Roses grow on stems full of thorns*. Does that mean we should concentrate on thorns and not notice roses? What need do we have for self-induced suffering or for empowering the suffering others try to inflict on us? And what need do we have of inflicting suffering on others? Fear not, there's plenty of suffering without creating more; the supply won't be seriously depleted. What we need as a remedy for the depression that can be caused by suffering, and as a safeguard for our sanity, is more self-induced empowering ourselves to enjoy life and more sharing of that enjoyment with others.

For there's plenty of joy around. As the intellectual-mystical American guru of the Fifties and

Sixties, Alan Watts, pointed out, "[T]he most acute and subtle joys of life…are…extremely common and simple." The problem is that we forget that this is so, and so we neglect to avail ourselves of them. Unlike suffering, which usually comes to us whether we invite it or not, joy is something we often have to go out of our way or make a conscious effort to find, for it waits for us and our ability and willingness to notice it or to create it, to receive its benediction, to allow its grace to help us, and to share its "good news" with others.

Sam and I travel on and wend our way slowly back to the windsurfing beach. I enjoy watching him find new scents and mark new boundaries for the ever-increasing domain of his summer territory. His pleasure is mine. For his joy, as always, is contagious. Not only is he my friend, he is my personal Alan Watts, my affectionate, faithful quadruped guru.

My most pleasant thought, my priority for the day, will help me to maintain, for awhile at least, the top vertical of the cruciform, the part that rises above the "thorns" of life, that transcends suffering. It has already greatly increased the domain of my happiness, a domain that only lacked a surveyor, that only lacked my willingness to become one with it.

I once wrote an excessive number of journal entries for a book that was to have been entitled *The Sad and Strange Crucifixion of Professor X*. Now I will sing another tune, one in harmony with Thoreau's early morning master of ceremonies and "master of all he surveys," the rooster:

WAKE UP—START ENJOYING LIFE!!!!!

# HOW TO CURE "HAVETOITIS"

"Havetoitis" is a widespread, little-recognized disease that causes the deterioration of billions of hours of human life every day. In some lives it may lessen the quality of one or two hours a day, in your own life of four or five hours of the twenty-four you are allotted, and in some lives of all sixteen, seventeen, or eighteen of the waking day. Multiplied by all the inhabitants of this globe, the total of "dis-eased" hours it causes is staggering.

Here's the way it insinuates itself into my daily life on a typical working day in the middle of a long winter, unless I am aware of it and take precautions against it. I am sure you can translate the following events into whatever situations are appropriate in your own life. Early in the morning, when I am sleeping better than I have slept all night, the alarm goes off, and I "have to" get up. Then I "have to" wash my face, and I "have to" brush my teeth, and, "oh, no, not again," I "have to" shave, and then I "have to" comb what's left of my hair. Then I "have to" make breakfast, and I "have to" wash the dishes. Now, I "have to" go out and face a cold, cold Colorado morning, and "have to" warm up the car, and "have to" remove the snow and ice from the windows, and "have to" drive to work. At work I "have to" finish preparations for my first class, and "have to" read over and comment on some student papers due to be returned at a later class, and "have to" advise a student or two, and "have to" answer a "memo," and then "have to" teach my first class. Need I go any further? Do I "have to?" I think you get the point. "Havetoitis" has already claimed the first three hours of my day, and the day has just begun.

But let's look at "havetoitis" for a minute as it affects you, not just daily, but throughout your life. Let's say that you are a college student, and let's pick up your "case history" at that point. It's highly probable that you consider yourself to be a victim of a "havetoitis," not-so-funny "sitcom" with endless episodes stretching before you, scripted with the following internal "have to" monologue: "I 'have to' take these classes, 'have to' study these books, 'have to' write these papers, 'have to' take these examinations, 'have to' prepare for a career, 'have to' obtain certain degrees." But, if this is the case, won't you subsequently "have to" get a job, "have to" do these particular chores on the job, "have to" fulfill all these particular obligations as a person with siblings, parents, and relatives, as a spouse, as a parent, as a grandparent, and so on, and so on, and so on? And won't this kind of thing continue until death finally frees you forever from a tedious existence that is just one "have to" after another?

If you enjoy suffering from "havetoitis," if it satisfies some masochistic need within you, if you wish to "live" your life only a few hours a week and think of the rest of your time as payment for those hours, then you don't "have to" read any further. If, on the other hand, you are even slightly disturbed about the deleterious effects of "havetoitis" in your life in the present or in the future, here are a few self-cures that might be of some help.

The most simple self-cure of "havetoitis" is the "verbal" one. Since the thought verbalized loudly or *sotto voce* in your mind in a significant number of situations is "I have to," why not consider substitute messages? As we all know, but rarely admit, *it's usually our attitude and not the specific event that causes our emotional response*—especially in the case of daily routine and how we feel about it. Why not, therefore, as an experiment, first "watch" yourself during a day or so and notice how many times you mutter out loud or to yourself—or simply feel the depressing effect of—"I have to." Just observing your "havetoitis" in action will start you on the road to recovery. Then for a day or two *substitute a healthier, life-affirming phrase for the old, time-murdering standby.* Some that I have tried and have found to be effective are: "I'm going to," "I choose to," "I want to," "I am privileged to be able to," "I like to," "Part of the time allowed to me on this earth I am devoting to," "I find it interesting to," "It will help me to grow as a person to," "There are a number of much more onerous tasks, but I am lucky to only be required to," and, even though it may sound extreme, "I love to."

If none of these phrases works, then stop thinking about yourself so much and *try a little altruism.* It won't hurt. As a matter of fact, it will probably help. If you can't convince yourself that the task at hand is not really so bad, or is even a lot better than you thought, think instead of how others will benefit from it. This is my favorite method for dealing with shaving, a daily routine I used to *loathe*. As I lather up and scrape away, I think about how my family, my students, and my fellow teachers will appreciate my clean-shaven

169

appearance. This makes the activity worthwhile and meaningful for me.

However, during the first years of my teaching career I didn't shave at all, and the only person I offended was my grandmother, who didn't like my Nineteenth-Century appearance. My students thought the beard and moustache looked professorial, even though they didn't approve of the way I pulled on the right side of my beard and twisted strands of it while involved in a discussion. So you see, I don't really "have to" shave. I choose to do so now, but I did not choose to do so then.

This brings us to another remedy for "havetoitis." *Maybe you don't "have to" do whatever it is you feel you "have to" do.* Many of the items on your "have to" list may be there simply because you have decided they "have to" be there. You could be wrong. And if you are, why not strike them from the list?

You may believe that in order to get along with a particularly outspoken and argumentative older member of your family you "have to" diplomatically hide your own feelings and opinions. Actually, the curmudgeon in question may relish a good "knock-down-drag-out" forensic battle, and your submissive, non-involved approach is making a better and livelier communication impossible.

Or you may have convinced yourself that you "have to" make lots of money in order to find happiness, and as a result "have to" pursue a career that is of little genuine interest to you. Both ideas may be wrong. Doing something else of more interest, even though it is less profitable, may be much more rewarding.

So it is with a number of "have to" situations. We are often mistaken about what we "have to" do.

The example about the career choice makes good sense, you might concede, especially if you're learning this "truth" the hard way. But what can you do, you might ask, if you've already invested in preparing for and are currently pursuing a career that you don't like? I would still suggest that you may not "have to" continue, even in this predicament. To begin with, you really didn't "have to" choose that career, or let it be chosen for you, did you? And if you are convinced that you've made the wrong choice, or that someone else made it for you, perhaps you can muster up the *courage* to make a change. Many others have done so.

However, if you insist on seeing yourself as being trapped by your commitments and obligations—and you may very well be seeing things clearly—then the least you can do for yourself and for everyone else around you is to stop chanting the mantra of self-flagellation and self-pity: "I have to," "I have to," "I have to."

Moving from *what* you do to *how* you do it, suggests another cure for "havetoitis"; namely, to perform the action, chore, or task at hand to the best of your ability without the interference of "have to" interior commentary. Rather than thinking "I have to do this," or even mentally drawing on a more positive substitute expression, *do it well. Do it with style, with grace.* Get out of your own way and let yourself enjoy your own skill in doing whatever it is you are doing. *There is a great pleasure to be derived from doing even the most menial task well.* So, if you're dissatisfied with *what* you are doing, perhaps you can find satisfaction in *how* you do it since YOU'RE GOING TO DO IT ANYHOW.

Furthermore, it's important to remember that everyone else around you is suffering from one form or another of "havetoitis." You may "have to" go to the dentist, and the dentist may "have to" extract your tooth, but the two of you do not "have to" find the experience unpleasant. You can talk to each other and thereby, through personalizing the situation, help alleviate one another's "havetoitis." Indeed, *the personal touch is great preventative medicine for many diseases of the psyche that increase unchecked when we feel that we are all alone, unappreciated, or unimportant.* That is why people prefer to go to and to work in offices where personal interrelations are as important as the services offered or the product produced. And that is why, if you bring the personal touch to whatever you "have to" do, you will find it much less tedious or trying.

Ah, but there's yet another remedy, desperate as it may be. It's known as curing the disease but killing the patient. I don't recommend it. But even a brief pseudo-medical treatise on a potentially deadly disorder such as "havetoitis" would be incomplete without the inclusion of extreme measures that have been taken to arrest its development. These measures are documented thoroughly in Herman Melville's short story about that very peculiar office clerk, Bartleby. Bartleby replaces the already toxic "I have to" with the much more poisonous "I prefer not to"; i.e., "I don't have to do anything, and therefore I *won't.*" True, he doesn't "have to" do anything, and, just as true, this anything eventually includes doing his work in the office, going home from the office at the end of the work day, eating to sustain himself, and even living itself, for Bartleby finally reaches the conclusion that he doesn't "have to" live.

It is interesting to observe that the disease and its most radical treatment are both deadly. The disease causes us to "just get through" life without "living" a large percentage of it; the extreme cure causes us to "get out" of life before we have experienced all of it. I would suggest that either extreme is to be avoided.

\*\*\*\*

There is no doubt that "havetoitis" can be cured, not entirely, but in a sufficiently effective way that can result in the reclamation of many more hours of "living" every day of your life.

Of course, you don't "have to" agree with me. Nor do you "have to" treat yourself for "havetoitis." It's your life, and whether you wish to be a "have to"

or not to be a "have to"
will "have to" be up to
YOU.

*Clay Boland Jr.*

# THE POSTERIOR APPROACH TO LIFE; OR, HOW VICARIOUS CAN YOU GET?

*...in remembrance of a former fraternity brother who flunked out of college after sitting in a large easy chair watching television nonstop for the first three months of his freshman year.*

THEY PLAY SPORTS FOR YOU,
WHILE YOU SIT IN YOUR CHAIR;

THEY PLAY MUSIC FOR YOU,
WHILE YOU SIT IN YOUR CHAIR;

THEY PURSUE ADVENTURE
AND TRAVEL AROUND THE GLOBE FOR YOU,
WHILE YOU SIT IN YOUR CHAIR;

THEY THINK FOR YOU
AND MAKE CONVERSATION FOR YOU,
WHILE YOU SIT IN YOUR CHAIR;

THEY'RE HAPPY FOR YOU, SAD FOR YOU;

THEY'RE GENTLE FOR YOU, VIOLENT FOR YOU;

THEY SING SONGS FOR YOU,
DANCE DANCES FOR YOU,
FALL IN AND OUT OF LOVE FOR YOU,

AND EVEN *MAKE* LOVE FOR YOU,
WHILE YOU SIT IN YOUR CHAIR.

ABOUT THE ONLY THINGS THEY CAN'T DO FOR YOU
ARE SLEEP, EAT, DRINK, ELIMINATE, AND, OF COURSE,
SIT IN YOUR CHAIR.

AND WHEN YOU DIE, OF PREMATURE *RIGOR MORTIS,*
THE MORTICIAN WILL HAVE NO CHOICE
BUT TO SOMEHOW OR OTHER EMBALM AND BURY
YOU
WHILE YOU SIT IN YOUR CHAIR
AND STARE...

AT NOTHING.

*Clay Boland Jr.*

# IMAGINATION

> *"Imagination is funny; it*
> *makes a cloudy day sunny."*
> —Johnny Burke

Imagine for a day that you are the star of a documentary film based on this one, particular, typical day in your life. Imagine that your name has been chosen totally at random, that the producers are on hand and ready—with their directors, interviewers, camera crews, various specialists, and even some yet-to-be-invented technology—to follow you everywhere you go, film everything you do, and record everything you say.

Imagine further that you will occasionally be asked to share your feelings about what you are doing, and that you will probably be asked questions about your motivation for doing whatever work you do, for your involvement in various activities, and for pursuing the lifestyle you have chosen.

Imagine how you would dress and groom yourself for this day. Imagine how you would want your room, your car, and your house—if you are lucky enough to have any of these—to look.

Imagine how you would participate in both your work and your leisure this day. Imagine how you would talk about the value of your activities in relation to the general scheme of things. Imagine any other comments you would make about your work, your relaxation, and your lifestyle, and about the choices you have made in your life that have determined what you are doing with your life on this particular day.

Most importantly, imagine how you would act with and react to all the people you meet during this day. Unless you're a hermit living in a cave, you'll be amazed when you realize how many people you interact with in the course of a single day, all of whom you affect one way or another, and all of whom affect you. Use your imagination to "preview" these interactions as you would like to have them happen in your documentary. For all the "scenes" and "sequences," imagine what you would do and say that would be different, that would show a part of you to the world that you are proud of. And, likewise, imagine what you wouldn't do and say, what would be omitted because it would show a part of you to the world that you would not like people to see.

Imagine the excitement and energy that would accompany you throughout that day, knowing that you were "on camera" every moment—as you get up in the morning, wash your face, see yourself in the mirror, have breakfast, go about your business, meet people, talk to people, go to lunch, finish your activities of the day, have dinner, spend the evening with friends or family, doing whatever you do that evening, and so on through the entire night until you wake up the next morning to start another day.

Imagine that this day of your life will be captured on film forever, and after having "rehearsed" it both mentally and emotionally as often as you can, live it accordingly.

****

If this experiment sounds interesting to you, give it a try. It may not turn you into a film celebrity, but it may help you to reassess your daily routine and discover *how to put more into it and thereby get more out of it.* It may give you a clearer perspective in regard to the many choices you have made in the past that have influenced "where" you are today—and lead you to other choices in regard to "where" you want to be in the future.

It may also help you to realize that you are involved every day of your life in a personally very important production called "A Day in the Life of..." And it may help you to understand that for yourself and for those who are in the production with you this ongoing "documentary" is of much more significance and consequence than you or they usually think it is.

If you like the results of this experiment, there is no reason not to try it again. *The more you let your imagination help you build and improve your self-image, the better.* The more you let your imagination help you perfect your career and personal skills, arrange your priorities, make whatever changes you need to make, and set your goals to be the kind of person you would like to see starring in each day's new documentary, the better.

\*\*\*\*

Remember too, that this "imaginative exercise" is an actuality as far as your brain is concerned, and will be stored within the "files" of your mind along with all the other "documentary films" of every day of your life, from your birth right up to the present. Some of these may be easier to access than others, but they're all there, and their overall content has much to do with how you think about yourself.

So, why not start putting more and more "daily documentaries" on the shelves that you like and would be glad to have others see?

Today, BE THE STAR YOU CAN BE.

Imagine the way you want to be, and you'll be on your way.

"Imagination *is* funny"; it can create reality.

So smile and imagine—"you're on [very] candid camera."

*Clay Boland Jr.*

# A ONE-WORD COURSE IN
# INTERPERSONAL RELATIONS

*Clay Boland Jr.*

# DOES ANYBODY LISTEN; DOES ANYONE CARE?

You know how hurt you feel, for we've all experienced it too often, when you've been talking to a friend about something personally important to you in order to get some sympathy, understanding, or support, and you get as your reply a comment on a totally different and unrelated subject. You say something about how hard you've been working or about the problems you're having with your "love" life, and your friend replies by starting a conversation about the weather, about buying a new pair of skis, or about what's happening this weekend.

You feel more alone than you felt before you tried to get some reaction to your concerns and feelings. And you begin to suspect that people may, indeed, be as cruel as many say they are, or even that the universe is as indifferent as you hoped it wasn't.

The only remedy is to *not* turn around and "listen" to someone else the same way.

*CRUELTY AND INDIFFERENCE ON THE ONE HAND, AND KINDNESS AND CARING ON THE OTHER, ARE BOTH CONTAGIOUS.*

*IT'S YOUR CHOICE AS TO WHICH YOU WISH TO PASS ON TO YOUR FELLOW HUMANS.*

Does anybody listen; does anyone care? Someone does if *you* do!

\*\*\*\*

The same principle applies throughout all of your life. If former, so-called "transgressions" against you have left you feeling alienated and bitter, for example, you are probably unable to see that you are not only a victim of the past (which you aren't willing to let die), but, more importantly, a perpetuator in the present of more of the same "transgressions" against others (whom you aren't willing to let live unless they "pay for" what others did to you). Venting your resentment on the innocent is uncalled-for, cowardly, and cheap. It also doesn't help you or anybody else. It drags us all down. It creates a "black hole" in everyone's social space.

Accept your lot, cut your losses, stop messing up other people's psyches, and get on with your life. *If you pass on, through your present resentment at "transgressions" against you in the past, what was done to you before, you're acting no better than those you claim have hurt you.*

Rather than passing on more of the same, pass on something better.

As Martin Luther King Jr. so aptly put it: "'An eye for an eye, and a tooth for a tooth' leaves everyone blind and toothless."

Does anybody listen; does anyone care?

I do.
You can.

And the more of us who do, the better.

# THE INDIVIDUAL IS NOT THE GROUP

> *"Human beings would...get along with each other better, and would approach each other more closely, were they able to understand one another better."*
> —*Alfred Adler*

The individual is not the group. The "group-person," who represents the embodiment of the group in other people's minds, exists merely as a myth but never as a reality. In reality no single individual in any group completely exemplifies the stereotype for that group, for the stereotype is a chimera not only of statistical dehumanization, but also of ordinary laziness, and—let us all confess—of extraordinary pride.

To save yourself the trouble of personal, in-depth inquiry, you let yourself learn to dislike, distrust, or even hate this "group-woman" and that "group-man." What you have learned to dislike, distrust, or even hate, however, is only *mythology,* and very often inferior and suspect mythology at that.

Get to know a real person, and more often than not you'll slowly come to realize that the individual you are dealing with is not a "group-person," but only one more individual *like* yourself, as real as yourself, and as "unstereotypical"—one more *of* yourself, whose group is *not a part of* but *all of* humankind.

# HOME

> *"All the world is sad and dreary ev'rywhere I roam."*
> —*Stephen Foster*

Looking at a Constable oil painting of an old thatched-roofed, cozy English cottage surrounded by the verdure of trees and hedges and the bright colors of cascades of flowers and vines which almost engulf it, we are reminded that the thing all "pictures" of home have in common is their misrepresentation of the truth. Home is a place that was—but never was as we remember and picture it in our minds; that is a certain way momentarily—but is constantly changing; that will be—but will not be the way we imagine.

Nevertheless, we constantly long for home, for the ineffable comfort of "being at home."

Most of us are too restless to want to stay at home, but *we all want a home* to at least come back to or at least visit now and then. However, few of us find it.

Why? Because we are unwilling to supply in our relationships, in our families, in our work, and even in our leisure, the *love* that creates it.

*Geography and architecture—and even vows and genealogy—do not make a home; the hard, unending, humble work of voluntary love—not the kind of love you fall in but the kind you give because it is needed—does.* And since most of us do not recognize this fact, we remain "homeless."

The hearth of the "home" is the patient, warm heart. And "welcome" means welcome to love given and received no matter what, means welcome to the sowing and reaping of life, whether the harvest is plentiful or bitter. *Home is wherever you create a home with love.*

But you cannot create such a "place" unless you are first "at home" with yourself: until you can LEARN TO ACCEPT YOURSELF AS YOU ARE RIGHT NOW, not as you hope to be; until you can LEARN TO ACCEPT YOURSELF AS YOU WERE, not as you wish you had been; until you can LEARN TO LOVE YOURSELF AS YOU WOULD HAVE OTHERS LOVE YOU; until you can learn to be "at home" with yourself as you would have others make you feel at home with them. And all of this "being at home with yourself" takes a lot of HUMILITY.

And you cannot create such a place unless you are willing to accept the shortcomings of others: until you can LEARN TO ACCEPT OTHERS AS THEY ARE RIGHT NOW, not as you hope they will be; until you can LEARN TO ACCEPT OTHERS AS THEY WERE, not as you wish they had been; until you can LEARN TO LOVE OTHERS AS THEY WOULD HAVE YOU LOVE THEM; until you can learn to be "at home" with others as others would have you make them feel at home with you. And all of this "being at home with others" takes a lot of CHARITY.

It is probably no coincidence that one of the most loved folk songs about home starts with the sentiment, "Be it ever so humble…"

It is probably no coincidence *that one* of the best known aphorisms about charity stresses the importance of learning it at home—where it has to begin if there is to be a "home," and if anyone is to have a chance to learn it.

****

Furthermore, it is probably no coincidence that America is undergoing an ever-growing problem of "homelessness" that is simultaneously both an actuality and a symbol of the greater "homelessness" that afflicts our society in the form of the replacement of the large, extended family unit that included grandparents, uncles, aunts, cousins, parents, and children with the much smaller nuclear family unit that sometimes contains two parents and their children, but more often only one parent and children or any of the possible regroupings of former broken marriages; with the exponential increase in delegation of parental responsibility to others; with the innumerable instances of unsatisfactory employment, periodic relocations, pervasive loneliness; and finally, and perhaps the most heartbreaking, the prevalence of substitute "havens" of alcohol and drug abuse sought by prodigal sons and daughters—as well as by their prodigal fathers and mothers.

And it is probably no coincidence that most people living on our planet are, despite all warnings, still in the process of destroying the only "home" that we have—due to their *lack of humility,* due to their unwillingness to accept our species as JUST ONE component of the whole interdependent biosystem, rather than the ONLY component of importance in it; and due to their concomitant *lack of charity* towards and impingement on the rights of all other life forms and natural phenomena on the planet.

Indeed, "homelessness" is already becoming a problem that is taking on greater dimensions than most people wish to acknowledge. Not only are vast numbers of people living in abject poverty throughout the year on the sidewalks and in the alleyways of our country's large cities, and thousands of people in displaced ethnic and national groups living in refugee camps throughout the world, but there are also very few Americans with houses and apartments to live in that experience the warmth and close-knitness of "home" in them that they need and desire. To say that entire populations are afflicted with "homelessness" is not overstating the case socially, politically, or metaphorically.

On the other hand, there are the "unafflicted"— those who live "beyond and outside the times." These are the adepts who are truly "at home" any place, any time, and under any circumstances. These are the few privileged wise people among us who, after learning to unconditionally accept themselves and others, have moved forward in their patiently developed and hard-earned humility and charity to see—as Hermann Hesse's Siddhartha finally does, his heart full of compassion and peace—beyond all *dualities* of good and bad, beneficial and evil, fair and unjust, to the *oneness* of the universe.

After all, that's what the word "universe" means: "oneness."

Be it ever so magnificent or incomprehensible, there's no place like it.

The rest of us could do a better job "being at home" in it.

## WE CAN START WITH OURSELVES AND OTHERS.

## GETTING OFF THE BENCH

> *"Help...[another's] boat across the river, and lo!— your own has reached the shore."*
>
> *—Hindu proverb*

I have found that the surest way to get help for your problems is to give help to others. Even if that help is minimal, such as showing an interest in what they are doing or what they think or how they feel, it gets you out of yourself and back out into the world beyond yourself. It gets you off the bench, where you have been sitting, silently sulking and feeling sorry for yourself, and back on the playing field where the real action is, where people work together as a team to try to win the game of daily life.

# TALENTS

> *"And being afraid I went and hid thy talent in the earth."*
>
> —*Matthew, 25:25*

Although the Twentieth Century began with most Americans being able to quote from the Bible, it will probably end with most of them not having read it, or even any part of it. This is unfortunate, for the Bible, which literally means "the book" (and throughout the last four or five centuries has been the Western World's best seller), contains many passages that offer valuable advice and wisdom. One does not have to be Jewish or Christian to benefit from reading its most famous sections, such as Psalms, Proverbs, Ecclesiastes, and the Gospels by Matthew, Mark, Luke, and John.

"The Parable of the Talents" is a good example of what I mean. It not only gives us the contemporary meaning of the word "talent" (a "talent" in Biblical times was simply a monetary unit based on a specific weight of a bag filled with gold or silver coins), but it also *gives us good advice on how to best fulfill ourselves and thereby achieve some of that elusive state called happiness.* It also warns us of the penalty for denying our natural abilities; i.e., our talents.

In the parable, the master leaves his three male servants with talents to invest in his absence.

When he returns, he naturally wants to know how each servant has done.

The first servant had been given five talents and has invested them wisely. "Well done, thou good and faithful servant," he is told.

The second had been given two talents and has invested them wisely. He is praised also.

Then the master turns to the last servant, who had been given only one talent.

This last servant confesses that, because he had been afraid, he hid his talent and made nothing of it.

The master is furious and sends him away in disgrace.

\*\*\*\*

The message of the parable is unequivocally clear. Each one of us is born with certain natural abilities; that is, each one of us receives the gift of particular talents. If we use these talents well, we can feel good about ourselves; we are *praiseworthy*. But if we deny what we can do best, we have denied our best abilities and feel *miserable* and "exiled."

It's interesting to note that the banished servant acted out of *fear*.

It's also interesting to note that the talent didn't belong to the servant, it was only *lent* to him.

The parable makes perfect psychological sense.

> IF YOU DO WHAT YOU CAN DO BEST,
> THEN YOU WILL FEEL FULFILLED;
> BUT IF YOU DENY
> YOUR NATURAL ABILITIES,

YOU WILL NEVER FEEL FULFILLED.

In choosing a career, then, think first about your strongest natural abilities and, if you can, find a vocation that employs them. The average person spends at least eight hours a day, five days a week, fifty weeks a year, for forty-or-more years, working. That's 8 times 5 times 50 times 40, and that equals 80,000 hours! You can choose to spend these hours doing what you do best, or you can hide your talents— out of fear of losing social status, parental approval, a large income, or whatever—and forever feel unfulfilled and dissatisfied because you are "alienated" from your potential.

It has become proverbial that in our society most people live for the weekends and dread returning to work Monday mornings. Most people's lack of devotion to their work was poignantly demonstrated by the college administrator who won the state lottery on television. When asked what was the first thing he would do now that he had won, his immediate reaction was: "Can I quit my job right here on television?"

Perhaps nobody *really* likes to *work,* but since you, like most of us, will probably find it necessary to do so, you can do a great favor for yourself and CHOOSE WORK THAT WILL LET YOU DO WHAT YOU CAN DO BEST.

For example, unless you have the talents necessary for business success and derive pleasure from the kind of work that brings it about, a large bank account or social prestige or comfortable conformity is sorry recompense for serving eighty-thousand hours of what will be for you empty time. Why sentence yourself?

What crime have you committed? *Life does not have to be a prison.* You do not have to be your own jailer. You don't have to go around wearing your social security number on a striped shirt as your identification.

Furthermore, what works best for you, works best for everyone else. For if you are realizing your true potential, you'll do good work, work that satisfies and helps others. The reverse of this is also true.

A modern retelling of the "Parable of the Talents" can be found in the movie, *Dead Poets Society.* A young prep-school student, whose father is a wealthy doctor, discovers that he has a remarkable talent for acting. He wants to investigate this talent and to even consider being a professional actor. His father, however, callously ignoring both his talent and his wishes, insensitively insists on forcing him into a medical career.

The final result is suicide.

It always is.

Either "short and sweet" or long and bitter.

TO DENY YOUR TALENTS
IS TO WASTE YOUR LIFE.

And *to waste your life is* certainly *a form of suicide.*

We all realize that artistic talents are often the hardest to make a living with, but the creator of the film story needed a heightened dilemma to make the point. It may be that some of your talents cannot "put bread on the table," but they can still be developed and enjoyed during many of the other sixty-thousand to eighty-thousand hours available to you when you aren't earning a "living," commuting, eating, or sleeping.

Many well-known composers and writers were men and women who pursued "double careers"—one that provided an income to support them, and one that provided an outlet for their artistic abilities. Alexander Borodin, the Russian composer, was a chemist by profession; Sir Arthur Conan Doyle, the English detective-story writer, was a doctor; and Emily Dickinson, the American poet, managed her father's household and dedicated much of her energy and time to caring for the sick and the dying in Amherst, Massachusetts. And the list goes on and on.

The number of famous people better known for their scientific, business, or political accomplishments than for their artistic pursuits is even larger. Among politicians, Winston Churchill and Dwight Eisenhower were very good amateur painters.

And, on the other hand, there have been professional artists, such as Rubens, and renowned musicians, such as Paderewski, who have demonstrated the ability to be effective politicians.

Also, a large number of people with artistic abilities have been able to use these abilities in related fields such as teaching, artist management, and publishing.

And many people with nine-to-five jobs participate in community theater, musical groups, and art competitions. Parallel examples can be given for people with athletic, social, and political talents. *Just because you can't make a living out of all of your talents doesn't mean that you can't make use of the ones financially unprofitable for you to help you, and others as well, enjoy living.*

And ideally, if you are or will be pursuing a "double career," you are or will be able to use your best abilities in *both.* For *your talents are neither as narrow in application as you think* (someone with a talent for architecture can express that talent in business organization) *or as few as you think* (hardly anyone is given just *one* talent as was the third servant in the parable).

*Nor are your talents bound by the perimeters of a job, a hobby, or a sport.* They are obviously part of achieving fulfillment in life, which should be your main occupation, although it is often the one most of us bring only our lesser talents and only a minimum effort to bear on, not realizing that OUR TRUE WEEKLY "PAYCHECK" IS NOT THE ONE THAT PAYS THE BILLS AND PUTS DINNER ON THE TABLE.

Should it be that you only need to match your talents to *one* "official" career, be sure to bring as many of them as feasible to the workplace in order to make your job as meaningful as possible. For instance, if you feel your interpersonal skills are equally as strong as the job skills you are hired to perform, you may still be able to use them in creating a mutually supportive atmosphere that improves the morale and efficiency of your co-workers.

Some talents may seem to be more "glamorous" than others, but I have observed that *people who use whatever talents they have been "gifted" with without worrying too much about fame or wealth are often far happier that those whose "glamorous" talents become burdens to them because they are unable to use them to gain the fame and wealth they wish.*

Whatever your talents are, appreciate them, use them well, share them with others, and stop looking for any more special favors. Accept what you have been given. GIFTS ARE MEANT TO BE ENJOYED AND USED, NOT COMPLAINED ABOUT.

Others may have received other gifts, and you may believe that they are luckier than you are, but in some very profound way that's none of your business. They have their lives to live and you have yours—both may be equally difficult. They have their talents and you have yours—both may be equally rewarding, unless you're determined to make things otherwise.

The main point is to *use the talents you have been given.* If you only have a few, make *more* out of less. If you have many, don't make *less* out of more. Don't hide your talents "in the earth" where they will do no good for you or anybody else.

If they are hidden now, find them, dig them up, invest them, and prosper. They are your true capital. They may not make you a fortune, but they can do something better, they can make you fortunate.

Smiley Blanton, in his book, *Love or Perish,* summed up the case very succinctly when he stated: "…all of us attain the greatest success and happiness possible in this life whenever we use our native capacities to their fullest extent."

Dr. Blanton should know. In his late twenties, he left the security of a successful college teaching career to enroll in medical school, for he felt medicine was his true vocation, his "calling." Rather than bemoan the fact that it was "too late" to spend years of study in preparation for a new career, he had the "stick-to-it-tiveness" to invest his talents and time wisely and to reap the dividend of a very rewarding life that benefited both himself and all the thousands and thousands of people who have read his books.

# "THERE IS NOTHING EITHER GOOD OR BAD, BUT THINKING MAKES IT SO"

"There is nothing either good or bad, but thinking makes it so." William Shakespeare said it. So have many others in other ways. The idea that the thought is parent to the emotion is an old one that has been reworked and rediscovered many, many times. However, since the idea is so regularly ignored, it might be worthwhile presenting it once more.

In general, except in the most drastic situations, we filter each event in our lives through our minds, placing each one on an evaluation scale that ranges from very pleasant to very painful. Our emotions, in turn, receive our mind's assessment of the event and supply the appropriate response.

An old anecdote might help make the point.

A poor farmer, the head of a Jewish family living in a rural Russian village, comes to the rabbi seeking help. He is distressed because he and his wife and his brother and his brother's wife and his cousin and his grandmother and several children of various ages, including a baby, are all crowded into a two-room hut. He is at his wit's end, for he considers the situation intolerable.

The rabbi tells him to take his goat into the hut as well.

The farmer is dismayed upon receiving this strange advice, but since he knows the rabbi is a wise man, he takes it.

A week later, the farmer returns in worse shape than before. The goat has been constantly bleating until nobody can bear the noise, has filled the hut with an unbearable stench, has managed to help itself to the family's food supply, makes the baby cry all day long, and has been chewing up much of the family's clothing.

The rabbi tells him to take his goat back out of the hut.

The farmer hurries home and removes the goat. Everybody eagerly helps clean up all traces of the goat's "interior redecoration" of their humble dwelling place.

Another week passes and the farmer returns, smiling and relaxed.

The rabbi comments that he seems to be much happier than when he first came to complain about his crowded house.

The farmer's rejoinder is that without the goat in the house life is wonderful.

The original *event* is still the same—the house is still crowded. The *thought* about the event, however, has changed. The resulting *emotion* is no longer disgust, bitterness, or sadness; it is the soothing serenity of relief.

The event, it is important to emphasize, is only a *fact*. In and of itself it is neutral. The *meaning* of the event is only possible through an interpretation. No interpretation; no meaning. The interpretation, in turn, is an "act of thinking." Therefore, the thought, not the fact, is the *cause,* and the emotion is its *effect.*

It is not necessary, however, to take a goat into your house to change the way you think about an event. The point is that you don't have to be "trapped" when faced with an event by the first thought that comes into your mind. In most cases, you can *choose* to think a different thought—other than the obvious and more destructive one—a thought that can help you keep your emotional equilibrium by evoking a positive response rather than a negative one.

And you can also consciously train yourself to do so through *the development of a healthy and realistic philosophy of life,* one which prepares you for most of the inevitable events that can happen to you, one which gives you an intelligent way to think about them and handle them *before* they occur. This kind of philosophical training is akin to the well-known "ounce of prevention" that can save you "a pound of cure," and, I might add, "a ton of grief" as well.

For instance, when you are criticized, you can think, "How dare this person point this out." Or, you can think, "I might learn something, so I'll listen." Or, you can think, "This person is being a true friend by trying to help me." The three possible emotions these three different thoughts would lead to are anger, patience, or appreciation. Furthermore, if your philosophy of life had already helped you to understand that criticism is essential to your personal development, and that *not* being willing to listen to criticism or learn from it "stunts your growth," you would not even have to make a conscious choice when in such a situation. We have all met those hapless people who at age forty are still unwilling to accept the criticisms that would have aided them at age fifteen. As a result, having yet "to grow up," they remain not forever young, but forever juvenile. Their reaction, still, to what they most need to hear, is both defensive and offensive.

But there is also a negative side to "thinking in advance"; for many unnecessary negative emotions come about from thinking not how things *might* be but from thinking in advance about how things *should* be. This approach to future events could rightly be labeled "private scenario" thinking. With your scenario in mind, you are ready to be upset by the first "script changes" the first actor or actress who doesn't follow your scenario makes—that is, unless the changes are an improvement on the original, for

MOST OF US *TALK* ABOUT "GOING WITH THE FLOW" BUT IN PRACTICE STAND IN THE RIVER, FACING UPSTREAM, AND TRY TO PUSH IT BACK. ALL WE MANAGE TO DO IS GET "ALL WET," AND SOMETIMES WE ALMOST DROWN.

You plan a hike but can't go because of a storm. You count on spending a weekend in the big city but can't get there because of car trouble or lack of transportation. You are sure you can impress a certain someone, and you fail. You think you can do well on a school or work assignment, but the opposite turns out to be the case. All or any of these put you in a tremendous funk.

They don't "have to."

You are not obligated to make yourself suffer this way.

You can think of these events in other ways. You can "change your mind" and avoid living from one negative emotion to the next, grinding your gears through life like a garbage truck constantly stopping to pick up more trash. You can *"change your mind" rather than* feel that it is necessary to *"escape your mind"* in order to experience positive emotions.

Right at this very moment, as you are reading these words, your mind may be assessing whether what you are reading is helpful, whether you should be doing something else, whether you should be somewhere else, whether you should be with someone else, and so on. But let your mind relax for a minute or two, and taking a deep breath…, think slowly and calmly:

"I can learn something from *everything.*"
"This is what I am doing."
"This is where I am."
"This is who I am with right now."

Get the message?

It is your *thoughts* that disturb you.

CHANGE THEM.

Your *emotions* will love you for it.

> "THERE IS NOTHING EITHER
> GOOD OR BAD,
> BUT THINKING MAKES IT SO."

# BUTTONS, BUTTON PUSHERS, AND ELEVATORS

 $T$ he metaphor of "pushing someone's buttons" probably implies that we all are like elevators. People can get a "rise out of us" by pushing *these* buttons; they can "bring or put us down" by pushing *those*. After enough trips in the elevator, they can push our buttons without looking and always get a predictable response. The elevator always goes to the "floor" requested unless others are joining in and pushing some of our other buttons as well. *Our buttons are pushed, and up and down we go.* In a true sense, we let others become our operators, some of them smooth and some of them rough. But it's not our fault. We're only elevators. Or are we?

The next time someone pushes one of your buttons, try responding in an unexpected way. For example, if you are an environmentalist and are attacked by a friend or relative who says there is no good reason to save a particular species that is endangered, rather than answer in outrage (the expected response), answer calmly, "You may be right." Or ask for further explanation and make a sincere effort to understand the other person's point of view. Or adroitly "short circuit" the "button push" by moving on to another aspect of the issue.

This is not a question of standing or not standing up for what you believe. Rather, I am asking you to become aware, and risking at the same time pushing one of *your* buttons, that you often act as if you were an elevator.

In some cases, therefore, it may be more important to prove that you aren't mechanical, pre-programmed, or easy to operate, to prove that you are not "abuser-friendly."

All problems, such as species' survival, and especially human species' survival, will never be solved by argument or even force if we all insist on being elevators.

Elevators cannot change their programming, their wiring, their buttons. Elevators cannot choose to *not* respond, nor can they choose to respond in new ways.

Of all the "isms" we are plagued with, "elevatorism" may be the worst. Or call it "Archie Bunkerism" if you prefer to honor the symbolic archetype of "elevatorism" that was created for commercial television. The fact remains that people seem forever divided because they too often become rigidly predictable, too inflexibly unable to rethink things objectively and in different ways.

*The issue isn't which religious, philosophical, political, economic, social, psychological, or personal view is the best. The issue is that thinking, responding, and acting in rigidly predictable and overly subjective ways is "endangerous."*

IN A WORLD OF ELEVATORS,
WE ALL END UP GETTING THE SHAFT.

# WHO SAID IT WOULD BE EASY?

> *"It is a great misfortune not to have experienced trials."*
> —Cicero

Nowadays one hears a lot about people's moral and personality problems being predominantly physical problems and therefore beyond the responsibility of the afflicted to cope with or remedy. Certainly, our mental institutions are proof that this is often the case for extremely disturbed individuals. And certainly, most moral and personality problems can probably be said to have some physical basis, especially in some of the more desperate cases of susceptibility to alcohol and drugs, and in particular when excessive alcohol or drug use or any similar excessive abuse of the body creates a self-destructive "habit," an artificially-induced "necessity" that the physiological system "learns" to crave. However, if this kind of thinking is taken too far, nobody will need to feel responsible for anything—except the members of the legal and medical professions hired to exonerate them. Perhaps it would be wiser to suggest that most moral and personality problems have a physical basis, but that nonetheless most normal people can learn to cope with the ones they "naturally" have by developing the *strength of character* needed to take responsibility for controlling them, and can manage to avoid the excesses that lead to artificially-induced additional ones.

The alternative is to find ourselves in the midst of moral anarchy and social mayhem. Worse yet, to hypothesize otherwise is to deny our human free will, a denial which those among us overwhelmed by moral and personality problems would find great relief in making, while throwing in (and not without some justification) environment, society, and education, along with physical causes, as the true perpetrators of their various "crimes."

Nobody could be foolish enough to deny that physiological factors, environmental factors, societal factors, and educational factors influence the behavior of the individual—these are constants in all people's lives. But it's extremely important not to overlook the variable in the equation—*the individual.* For the individual has more than a little to say and do about how all these factors interact and how they are overcome or given into, used to advantage or disadvantage, countered or countenanced, and transcended or embraced.

To focus in on the physical factor will make the case for the others, for it is, with certain exceptions such as the environmental ones of extreme poverty and crime-ridden neighborhoods, probably the most powerful one on the list. Further, to simplify the physical case to one physical drive that is universal, let's talk about *sex.*

The "sex drive" is basically physical in origin, though we add much of the psychological and imaginative to it, and although it has a definite effect (as does any other basic physical drive) on individual emotional, mental, social, and spiritual development—just as individual emotional, mental, social, and spiritual development, in turn, has a definite effect on the role that sex plays in our lives, and how we deal with it, and how it affects our personalities. For some, and at certain times, sexual activity is more physical than emotional; for some, more emotional than physical. And for yet others, sexual activity can involve several experiential levels, or even all aspects of the personality, including the spiritual.

Whatever the individual variation, at any given time, on the very popular theme called sexuality, I would venture to say that there is no other commonly shared physical drive that causes more untold moral and personality problems for almost everybody than this particular biological imperative. Indeed, it might not be going too far to say that obsession with the sex drive is a universally available "addiction," capable of being just as powerful as the addiction to alcohol or drugs (and often, it might be possible to consider, probably the preliminary addiction leading to the abuse of these substances); and it might not be going too far to say that almost everyone who has ever lived and everyone who is living has been or is a potential victim.

And yet, despite its universal popularity, and the strong physical impetus that leads us to eagerly participate, all moral writers of all ages and all cultures have urged us to control the sex drive, to keep it in perspective, to incorporate it intelligently in our lives, and to accept the full responsibility of doing so.

Well, sometimes it's easy to believe that all moral codes were written by the Tartuffes of this world, or by people with ice water instead of blood in their veins, or, in this particular case, by eunuchs. That is, until you go out and test their theories by ignoring their advice. Then you discover that they too must have learned the hard way and turn out not to be as mistaken as you believed they were.

Remember, even though some of the more fanatic among them suggest total abstinence, the more realistic among them suggest *moderation and control, the proper circumstances,* and *the proper motives*—all of which are quite different than the denial of a very insistent and persistent physical drive. Ironically, since these precepts help you build character and help you feel more in control of your life, they help you *"feel good"* in a different and in a longer lasting way—good about yourself.

Moreover, since these teachings assign the joyous privilege of sex to its appropriate place in a "balanced" life, they make of it a blessing rather than a curse.

Despite the fact that the struggle to conquer and channelize the sex drive is extremely difficult for many of us and seems at many times nigh impossible and even "unprofitable" because of the tremendous expenditure of energy and effort needed; and despite the fact that this biological imperative challenges many of us most of our waking hours and "attacks" many of us nightly during our sleeping hours, often making it difficult to enjoy untroubled rest or "sweet dreams"; we would lose all dignity and respect for ourselves if we didn't make the effort to control and sublimate this physical urge—even if our efforts often end in failure.

And that is why I am tired of hearing all this cowardly cant about placing responsibility on everything and everybody but "the party of the first part" simply because it is difficult to deal with physical predispositions (unless, of course, the predisposition in question is pathologically beyond personal remedy). *It is difficult to deal with them, and we all have them.* That's part of life, but certainly *not all* of it.

We all have our physical predispositions towards various weaknesses and obsessions. Some have more of this, some have more of that; some have a small portion of many, and some a large portion of one or two. And *the ones you don't have and don't suffer from seem abstract and absurd to you.* And *the ones you do have seem abstract and absurd to your friends who don't suffer from the same predispositions.* To someone somewhat lazy, the workaholic seems totally strange; to the person with a voracious appetite, the frugal eater seems to be a creature from another planet. However, for one and all of us, dealing with the predispositions we have is always difficult; it is always hard. It always involves anguish and suffering. It always involves "starting over" and "starting over" again. It always involves new resolutions or old ones made again, and again. It always involves lots of lonely struggle, although most people are considerate enough not to bother others by complaining about it.

\*\*\*\*

Whether people talk about it or not, *dealing with personal adversity is part of our lot.*

*Adversity is our enemy, but adversity is also our friend,* our strength; for in preparing for combat and fighting in battle we grow strong. And as has been suggested in many ways by many wisdom writers, *the greatest heroes are those who have the fortitude, discipline, and endurance to conquer themselves.*

The military imagery is fitting. The best thing that can be said about war is that it is a perfect metaphor for one of the major challenges of being human.

But continuing the metaphor and getting back to sex, I'm not at all adverse to having some quality rest and relaxation now and then—it's absolutely imperative. We all need a little now and then. I do. You do. Just don't expect an everlasting peace.

Who said it would be easy?

"War is hell."

It's very difficult.

It's very hard.

Always.

But *victory is sweet,* and *peace sublime.*

# SANCTUARY

The 1990 edition of *Webster's New World Dictionary,* Third Edition, presents the word "sanctuary" as being etymologically derived from the Latin adjective *sanctus,* which means "sacred." And it offers as its two main definitions:

> "1) a holy place; specif[ically], a church, temple, etc.[; and]
> 2) a place of refuge or protection[.]"

We are familiar, from watching movies made in the earlier years of Hollywood on late-night television, with the use of cavernous, metropolitan cathedrals as places of protection for fugitives from the law and for others seeking personal asylum from those who would do them violence. This use of the word "sanctuary," however, is a very limited one, and, indeed, is only a *secular* one at that. I would like to attempt to restore the primary meaning of "sanctuary" and extend its metaphorical implications in order to reestablish the idea of sanctity given in that primary meaning and to emphasize the importance, for everyone, religious or non-religious, who wishes to remain *compos mentis,* of finding at least one personal "sanctuary" from the pressures of living in this loony bin, this bizarre phenomenon called the world, to which we all have contributed our own irrationalities and to which we all have been committed for life.

The classic film, *The King of Hearts,* ends with its hero seeking his "sanctuary" from the world in a local mental institution, for he has concluded from his participation in World War I that the world outside its walls is crazier and more destructive than the one within. This is a desperate remedy, but, in the context of the gruesomeness, mindlessness, and incredible carnage of World War I, it is perhaps the only chance the ex-soldier has of retaining his sanity. I do not wish to suggest a "sanctuary" this extreme, even though many cultures, such as those of the American Indians, have considered their "crazies" as being, in a special sense, and by being out of their senses, holy people, safe in their own personal sanctuaries.

Webster's helps in the reestablishment of the sanctity of "sanctuary" through its definition of "holy," the key word used in the definition given for "sanctuary," for the dictionary suggests that "holy" evolved from the Old English *halig* and means:

"1) dedicated to religious use; sacred
  2) spiritually pure; sinless
  3) deserving deep respect, awe, etc."

It is also helpful to record the dictionary's entry for "refuge," which is given as:

"a shelter or protection from danger, difficulty, etc.[,]" its Latin roots being "*re*, back + *fugere*, flee. "

These definitions and derivations are useful in accurately determining the exact denotation and connotation of a "place" we all need to "visit" frequently if we are to find any sanity or solace in the midst of a world whose inhabitants often seem to be crazier than the inmates of that notorious old London mental hospital of St. Mary of Bethlehem (the abbreviation of the hospital's name to simply "Bethlehem" and the reduction and corruption of those three distinct Hebrew syllables to two slurred Cockney syllables which added the word "bedlam" to our language, a word defined as "any place or condition of noise and confusion").

Combining all this lexicographical information in synopsis form qualifies "sanctuary" as being a "place" that protects and shelters us from the dangers, noise, difficulties, and confusions of life, and that does this by the salubrious, regenerative, and perspective-readjusting effect we experience from being in the presence of that which evokes our spiritual respect and concomitant *devotion;* i.e., the accompanying "mixed feeling of reverence, fear, and wonder" that we call "awe."

The presence of "fear" in this synoptic definition may seem to contradict the idea of comfort one would expect to find in a sanctuary. However, this "fear" is a "holy" fear and has to do with being in the presence of spiritual power we cannot fully comprehend. Therefore it is an *edifying* fear, one that "instruct[s] so as to improve or uplift morally."

Although there are many "lesser sanctuaries" that you can find in life—and that are more in keeping with the *secondary and secular* meaning of the word, such as walking the dog, talking to a good friend, or being totally absorbed in your work—I believe that without at least one "quintessential sanctuary" in your life, you are more than likely to be prematurely overwhelmed, discouraged, and defeated by "the dangers, noise, difficulties, and confusions" that pursue everyone of us individually and all of us collectively.

Moreover, I believe that this "sanctuary," if it is to be effective, should be one that calls for your active involvement in "creating" it, even if your "sanctuary" is achieving the passive detachment of meditation. For your participation helps you "get out of yourself," helps you "flee" momentarily from all the "dangers, noise, difficulties, and confusion" you normally inflict on yourself in your daily involvement with life.

I also believe that your "sanctuary" should ideally be one that is individually available almost anywhere, under almost any circumstances, to almost anyone, at almost any age, who is willing to make the effort to find it and become actively involved in "creating it." Such a "sanctuary" won't be suddenly unavailable to you one day simply because you're unable to actively participate in it due to the loss of friends or of loved ones, or due to growing older, being in bad health, or losing some particular physical ability. Indeed, if your choice doesn't fit most of these qualifications, it is more than probable that you have chosen a lesser and less effective "sanctuary" as your "sacred place and refuge," if only for the mere fact that it is less reliable and has "too many strings" attached to it.

And what are some of the more obvious, universal, "quintessential sanctuaries" available to just about everybody?

The closest to the original *literal* sense of "sanctuary" as being a "holy place" would be "a church, temple," cathedral, mosque, monastery, or any other structure inspired by the religious impulse. To enter such a structure, even for the "non-believer," is both a "leaving-the-world-outside-the-doors" and an enchanted entrance into a momentary Shangri-La, into the timeless ambience that transcends all petty, ephemeral concerns and the soon-to-be-only-dimly-remembered current events of the passing parade of history. But to enter such a structure and participate there through prayer, singing, and the receiving of instruction is to add the needed "active involvement" that converts any religiously inspired structure into a true "holy place and refuge," into a true sanctuary.

Moving from the literal to the *metaphoric* suggests that "sanctuary" can be found in religious devotions regardless of actual "place," or in any activity that serves a similar "sacred" purpose. For instance, meditation is a form of devotion recommended by many religious groups and is usually practiced outside official structures in any place the practitioner can find or create the prerequisite silence and solitude. Likewise, the study of religious writings, an important part of most religions, can often be done in the privacy of one's home. Throughout much of the American experience of the 1600's, the 1700's, the 1800's, and the early 1900's, the evening family bible reading was the main daily "sanctuary" available to most of the population, their shelter from the "dangers, noise, difficulties, and confusion" of pioneer and frontier living.

"Sanctuary" can also be found in active involvement with great artistic works—more obviously with great religious literature (as the example of the family bible implies), great religious music (which includes great hymns and great orchestral and choral works), great religious paintings (which can be found in many art museums and places of worship), and great religious sculpture and architecture (which are two of the main attractions of tourist "pilgrimages" in Europe)—but also through active involvement with *the masterpieces of literature, music, painting, sculpture, and architecture that celebrate the spiritual within us,* even though these exceptional works have not been specifically labeled as being religious.

Personally, I find the study, practice, and performance on the piano of the works of the great "serious" composers—in particular the best keyboard works of Bach, Beethoven, Mozart, and to a lesser extent, Chopin—to qualify on all counts as a "quintessential sanctuary." This past year I have found great comfort and inspiration in devoting an hour every evening possible to learning and playing the twenty-four pairs of preludes and fugues of Bach's *Well-Tempered Clavichord, Book I,* and applying myself also to gaining competency in performing his *Two-Part Inventions* and *Three-Part Inventions.* Although these works are nominally secular, one has only to hear them to know that they are actually profoundly *spiritual*—not only because of their *content* but also because of their perfect *form.* The economy, power, and emotional range of thematic materials and the kaleidoscopic variety and intricacy of their formal development almost always fill the performer, the musicologist, and the listener with "awe."

As in all art, both *content* and *form* act upon the "audience." So, in *spiritual* art the more "perfect" both content and form are, the more they partake of the perfection of any of the innumerable and marvelous phenomena of nature, such as a magnificent summer sunset, the brilliance of a forest arrayed in autumn colors, or the ebb and flow of the eternal ocean; and the more therefore they inspire in us that wonder and admiration for that which we, and even the writers, musicians, and artists themselves, can appreciate but never totally comprehend.

In brief, *the experience of perfection in both content and form* that can be found in the best and most noble works of music, literature, and art *is to a great extent a mystical one* that offers us renewed wonder every time we avail ourselves of it.

Furthermore, *these miraculous "uplifting" works are inspired* (the human "creator" acting merely as a "channel") *and,* in turn, are *inspiring.* For, through notes, words, color, and design, these works not only awaken mystical intimations of the inexpressible, but also encourage our highest aspirations, our best qualities, and the most noble potentialities within each of us. The ancients called this mysterious and ennobling power *psychagogia.*

The ancients, for the same reason, made active participation in the understanding, performance, and writing of music and poetry essential parts of education. But in an age in which we have delegated others to play musical instruments for us, to sing and dance for us, and also write lyrics and poems for us, I would not be surprised if you were to object that my "sanctuary" of studying and playing Bach is not available to you or to many of your friends.

However, it is not necessary to be a musician, writer, or artist in order to be "actively involved" in music, literature, or art.

For example, undisturbed "active listening" to great classical music can be extremely *edifying* and can offer you a "place" of wonder and awe and refuge to visit frequently. The most ideal place for such listening would be a symphony hall, but you can create the isolation and freedom from disturbance needed in your own home by using a set of headphones plugged into your electronic music source and closing your eyes to all outside distractions

In literature, you can find "sanctuary" in the study of writers such as Homer, Sophocles, Shakespeare, Cervantes, Dostoyevsky, Tolstoy, Conrad, Joyce, and Mann; in the reading of anthologies of great poetry; and in the investigation of wisdom writings such as Marcus Aurelius' *Meditations,* Henry David Thoreau's *Walden* (which I have drawn on more than once in this little handbook), and J. N. Krishnamurti's *Think on These Things.* The challenge involved, as in the case of listening intelligently to "serious" music, if accepted, will more than reward you with a "sanctuary." It will also greatly expand your understanding of the human condition, and help you to live your life more fully and more richly.

Visiting art galleries (or borrowing books of great art from the library) and becoming a student of great art would be another means of creating a personal "sanctuary" in the midst of the turmoil and perturbations of this world. Introducing yourself to the masterpieces of DaVinci, Brueghel, Bosch, El Greco, Caravaggio, Velasquez, Monet, and Van Gogh will be both edifying and broadening, and will teach you new ways to see and feel and think.

And seeking the "solitude and silence" of nature, the greatest art gallery of all, the gallery that is all around you, the gallery that you can find even in a city park, also affords yet another "sanctuary," if not the greatest of all, the one most available for all, and perhaps the most effective of all because it "speaks" eloquently without needing the aid of expert exegesis or exposition.

The study of any of the marvelous phenomena of nature can also be a "sanctuary," for whether you study astronomy, biology, chemistry, physics, geology, kinesiology, or anatomy, you will find a higher perfection of content and form than that found in the greatest artistic productions of humankind, a perfection that cannot help but fill you with admiration and amazement.

Even the study and skillful use of language, which is the study and application of another "miraculous" phenomenon, can act as a "sanctuary," for speaking, reading, and writing, which are our species' unique endowments, are "miraculous gifts," and their development is the result of the collective imaginative and inventive endeavors of countless generations. With this "sanctuary" this essay began, and it is appropriate that it ends with a tribute to the wonder of language, a wonder that deserves our "deep respect."

Find your sanctuary—whether it be one of the many suggested here or another (such as one that comes from contemporary art, music, or literature) that brings about the same results for you. Develop your "active involvement" in that sanctuary, and let it help you retain your sanity in the midst of an insane world.

Better yet, find more than one.

WITHOUT SOME HOLINESS IN YOUR LIFE, YOUR LIFE IS NOT WHOLE, FOR YOU PAY NO REVERENCE TO THE MIRACLE OF YOUR OWN EXISTENCE AND THAT OF OTHERS OR TO THE MIRACLE OF ALL THE WONDERS THAT EXIST AROUND YOU.

Without some sanctuary in your life, you will never know anything but "danger," "noise," "difficulty," and "confusion."

Bedlam is the state of the world; sanctuary is the way to survive it.

Uninterrupted bedlam without a personal sanctuary to turn to is a good regimen for ending up in a straightjacket; just as a personal sanctuary that serves as a readily available "leave of absence" from bedlam is a good prescription for maintaining your spiritual, mental, and psychosomatic well-being.

LIFE IS SACRED.
EXISTENCE OF THE UNIVERSE AWESOME.
DON'T BE PROFANE.
HALLOW THE DAY.
EVERY DAY.
THERE IS
NOTHING
"EVERYDAY"
ABOUT IT.

# ON SEEING VOYAGER TELEPHOTOS
# OF THE MOONS OF URANUS

WE EXPLORE ALL THE INTRICATE WONDERS
OF OURSELVES,
OF THIS PLANET,
THIS SOLAR SYSTEM,
THE UNIVERSE,

FILLING ENDLESS BOOKS AND DOCUMENTS
AND FILES AND TAPES
AND RECORDS AND FILMS
WITH OUR FINDINGS.

AND YET,
THE SMALLEST MICROBE
AND THE LARGEST GALAXY
ARE EQUALLY BEYOND
OUR
TOTAL
COMPREHENSION.
WE CAN EXPLAIN, ALMOST,
HOW EVERYTHING WORKS
BUT NOT EXACTLY,
IN THE LAST ANALYSIS,
WHY.

ULTIMATELY, WE REACH A PLACE OF NO ANSWERS,
A PLACE WHERE OUR QUESTIONS
HAVE NO MEANING,
A PLACE OF SILENCE,
A PLACE OF AWE.

223

# ENTHUSIASM

Enthusiasm, an infectious state of being with which we are all familiar (and which should not be confused with "mindless excitement," such as demonstrated in cheerleading), has a literal meaning that surprises most people, for it literally means "the expression of the God within."

I don't believe that anyone will ever adequately define the concept "God." How can one express the inexpressible? I do believe, however, that most of us feel that the world and everything in it, including ourselves, and everything surrounding it—the other planets, the sun, the moon and the infinite number of stars and galaxies that fill the celestial night—is *miraculous*.

Various people in various cultures and from various time periods have used various terms to try to convey in words their awe, appreciation, and even their fear of creation and their willingness to attribute its wonders and mysteries to many creators or to just one.

For most of the orthodox religious there are either a number of Deities (if their orthodoxy promotes polytheism) or only one Deity (if their orthodoxy has made them monotheists). And members of some religious systems refuse to name the "Un-nameable." For yet others, who feel a spiritual kinship with all of humankind and with all of creation, but who do not espouse any of the conventional religions inherited from earlier stages of the development of our species, the concept of "God" may be the "Cosmic

Consciousness" that they perceive as dwelling in and thereby linking together all people, which is both the universal spirit that animates and the universal power that creates.

On the other hand, for atheists, it may be simply Circumstances or Chance that have or has brought about the results we call the universe. And for agnostics, such may be the case, or there is a possibility that some Force might be credited—but they *doubt* anybody's ability to determine which of the many theories believed in is correct.

Whatever metaphor or metaphors people use to express their belief or non-belief, the majority of people who have lived have felt and believed, and the majority of those living still feel and believe, that being in touch with that which is represented by whatever name or names or "no-name" they use to express the inexpressible is of ultimate importance.

For these people, to be filled with "divinity" is to be truly alive.

And hence our word "enthusiasm" which tells us of the life-giving energy found by finding within ourselves and expressing in all that we do the joy and wonder of being in touch with that which creates and animates all.

Oddly enough, I have sometimes found amazing enthusiasm in people who claim to be atheists or agnostics; and, alas, I have sometimes found enthusiasm totally lacking in people who can quote every chapter and verse of the sacred texts of their various religions.

But *I have found the most enthusiasm of all in those people*—both officially religious and officially non-religious—*who give of themselves to others:* in doctors, in teachers, in members of religious orders, in loving parents, and in many outgoing, encouraging people of all ages in all walks of life. Their enthusiasm shines in their faces and inspires all those around them. It is contagious.

Whatever all these people are in touch with and are expressing, it's wonderful.

We can't have too much of it.

And better yet—it's *within* each of us waiting to be used.

Whether we use it or not, it's always there.

It's a "salvation" *accessible to everyone* regardless of creed or lack thereof.

Access it.

Tap into its creative power.

IT MAY BE AS CLOSE
AS ANY OF US WILL EVER GET
TO EXPRESSING
THE INEXPRESSIBLE
IN OUR LIVES.

## SPEAK YOUR DAYS WITH COURAGE

SPEAK YOUR DAYS WITH COURAGE,
ACT THEM WITH HELPING,
LIGHTEN THEM WITH HUMOR.

SING YOUR DAYS WITH GRATITUDE,
DANCE THEM WITH GRACE,
CELEBRATE THEM WITH AFFECTION.

THE LOVE YOU ARE LOOKING FOR
IS TO BE FOUND
IN SHARING IT.

*Clay Boland Jr.*

# ABOUT THE AUTHOR

Clay Boland Jr.

Clay Boland Jr. is a retired Colorado Mountain College Professor of Communications and Humanities. This handbook is the culmination of years of diverse life and work experiences and twenty-six years as a full-time teacher of an eclectic variety of college courses, including literature, philosophy, interpersonal relations, art, and music.

He also created and directed the Humodyssey program, a two-year interdisciplinary course of studies for freshmen and sophomores funded by the National Endowment for the Humanities, a program praised by both students and visiting professors from various universities.

His desire is to help readers of this handbook find more meaning and fulfillment in their own daily "ordinary living," and also contribute more to the quality of life of those around them.

He lives in Colorado with his wife Mary, and spends time with his two grown daughters and two grandchildren. In addition, he keeps busy with his many interests, including music (he's an accomplished jazz pianist), gardening, windsurfing, kayaking, sailing, hiking, cross-country and downhill skiing, and traveling.

www.ingramcontent.com/pod-product-compliance
Lightning Source LLC
Chambersburg PA
CBHW030304290526
45785CB00001B/212